Choosing Quality Child Care

How to Be Confident You Make the Right Choice.

The American Red Cross Search Guide

American Red Cross

©1999 The American National Red Cross

Revised 2001

Developed by the Badger Chapter of the American Red Cross

All Rights Reserved.

This guide, or parts thereof, must not be reproduced in any form without the expressed written consent of the American Red Cross, Badger Chapter.

Printed in the United States of America

To order, or for more information, please contact:

American Red Cross
Badger Chapter
4860 Sheboygan Avenue
P.O. Box 5905
Madison, WI 53705
(608) 233-9300 ext. 253
FAX: (608) 233-8318
customerservice@arcbadger.org

THE AMERICAN RED CROSS HAS APPROVED
American Red Cross
NATIONAL HEADQUARTERS
REGISTRATION NUMBER: 49064-93
EXPIRATION DATE: 11/01/02
THIS ITEM FOR NATIONWIDE DISTRIBUTION

Acknowledgments

Many child care professionals, American Red Cross staff, parents and volunteers contributed their expertise and ideas toward the development of the American Red Cross *Choosing Quality Child Care* guide. Without their support, energy and enthusiasm, this guide would not have been developed with such high quality or in such a timely fashion.

(Stock #19914)

Choosing Quality Child Care
Search Guide Outline

Part A: Before We Get Started

Purpose of the Guide 1

Objectives 1

Part B: Choosing Quality Child Care

Section I: Getting Started: Introduction and Orientation 3

Beginning a Successful *Choosing Quality Child Care* Search 3

Defining Child Care from Your Perspective: Activity #1 5

Section II: Introducing the Types of Child Care and Financing 7

Types of Child Care 7

Finding Dollars for Child Care 11

Defining Your Preferences: Activity #2 16

Section III: What are the Indicators of "Quality Child Care"? 19

Licensing 20

Accreditation 22

Section IV: Finding Quality Child Care in Centers and Family-based Care 24

An Overview of the Search Process 25

The Search Process: Step 1, Research Your Options 29
        🚌 Resource List: Activity #3

The Search Process: Step 2, Telephone Inquiry 35
        ☎ Telephone Questions

The Search Process: Step 3, Interview Providers and Centers 39
        🛝 Interview Providers & Centers Outline

The Search Process: Step 4, Take a Tour 44
        🏠 What-to-look-for Guide

The Search Process: Step 5, Observe the Program in Action 49
        👓 Observe the Program in Action Checklist: Activity #4

The Search Process: Step 6, Put It All Together:
        Select The Finalists and Make Your Decision 57
        🌼 Put-it-all-together Key

The Search Process: Step 7, Evaluate 61
        📄 Evaluation Form

The Quick Search. 65

Section V: Finding Quality Child Care: The Search for In-home Care 66

An Overview of the Search Process 66

The Search Process: Step 1, Research Your Options 67
Resource List

The Search Process: Step 2, Interview Providers and Invite Them to Visit Your Home 71
Interview Providers

The Search Process: Step 3, Telephone References. 75
Checking References of In-home Providers

The Search Process: Step 4, Select the Finalists and Make Your Decision 79
Put-it-all-together Key

The Search Process: Step 5, Evaluate 83
Evaluation Form

Section VI: Wrapping It All Up 87

Finding and Selecting Quality Child Care is Just the Beginning 87

The hopes and fears…the unwillingness to compromise…for many parents, an essential part of life is child care. We understand what you are going through. That's why your local American Red Cross chapter is offering you a *Search Guide* for *Choosing Quality Child Care.*

Part A: Before We Get Started

Purpose of this Guide

The primary purpose of this guide is to assist you in making child care choices that best meet the needs of your individual circumstances. The guide covers basic information about the types of child care available as well as useful information about licensing and accreditation, financing child care, and a thorough overview of the search process.

Guide Objectives

After reading this guide, you will be able to:

- Identify and express your hopes and concerns about child care

- Identify and understand regulations governing child care including licensing and accreditation

- Identify policies and practices you should seek when choosing child care

- Define your child care needs and preferences

- Identify and understand the elements that comprise quality child care

- Identify the characteristics of a quality child care provider by asking questions and through observation

- Use educational materials such as checklists to locate quality child care

- Identify health and safety issues in child care

- Learn what questions to ask—and to whom to ask them—when interviewing child care providers about a child care program

- Learn how to put all the elements together to make a decision on choosing quality child care for your child

- Learn how to conduct ongoing evaluation of the child care you select.

This booklet contains all the materials and tools you will need to increase your knowledge, skills and confidence!

In reaching a final decision, you will need to weigh factors such as cost, location, availability (openings), quality of care, compatibility with your values and the temperament of your child. It is an exciting decision to make and an important one.

Section I: Getting Started. Introduction and Orientation

Section I Goal Statement: When you have completed this section, you will be familiar with the goals of the American Red Cross *Choosing Quality Child Care* guide.

You will also:

■ become familiar with guide objectives, structure and content

■ identify your expectations, concerns, and issues related to child care and the search for quality child care

■ define what quality child care means to you

Welcome to the Beginning of a Successful Choosing Quality Child Care Search

Being a parent is a challenging and rewarding job. Finding quality care for your child is one of the most important duties you will perform as a parent.

Parents must make many critical decisions about how their children will be raised. These decisions relate to sharing of family values, the friends children will have and special interests they will pursue. Your role as a parent is to make the best possible decisions for your child and your family. Choosing quality child care is one of these important decisions.

Child care is a fact of life for millions of American families. Each workday more than 25 million Americans with children under age 6 leave their children in someone else's care. There are many choices out there, and we will help you choose carefully.

The big questions, of course, to ask are:

■ What do I look for?

■ What do I ask?

■ When do I start looking?

■ How do I find what I want?

Finding quality child care really boils down to the "Three Ps" of child care: the **place**, the **program** and the **provider**. These "Three Ps" will come up again a little later.

After completing this guide, you will have the knowledge and the tools to make an informed decision about choosing quality child care.

■ You will learn that not all child care programs are equal in quality.

Part B: Choosing Quality Child Care

■ You will learn how to evaluate one provider or child care center compared to another.

■ You will learn important insights about what to look for and what to ask when you visit prospective child care providers or centers.

Through this self-study you will define your child care needs—an early, vital step in choosing quality child care. This guide is the "road map" that helps you determine what you are seeking in child care. Further, it helps you identify the qualities that comprise quality child care.

Different Things to Different People

Making a child-care choice is a personal issue. Your neighbor's need for child care may be markedly different than yours. The special characteristics that make every person and family unique also make their need for child care a unique responsibility.

How do you personally define what "child care" means? This is an important exercise because it will help you establish what you are looking for. In fact, once you've defined what child care means to you, it is much easier to not only identify it but to find it.

One of the best ways to describe exactly what child care means to you is by completing Activity #1.

Please take a few minutes now to fill in the blanks for each item 1-4.

1. friendly staff
   engaging activities
   clean, orderly place
   ok neighborhood
   security process
   structure, sense of
   routine
   knowledgeable staff
2. I feel safe
   ~~variety~~ multicultural

2. minds at ease
Kat becomes comfy
Kat makes friends
meet other parents

3. positive
enjoy her time there
safe

4. We'll hate it
easy personality ↓
negative / bad exper.
she'll be mad 4ever

Defining Child Care
From Your Perspective

Child care means different things to different people. Your definition may also change as you work through this guide.

Please take a few minutes to complete the questionnaire below. Once you have defined child care, what you expect to receive from it and fears or reservations you have about it, you can then seek child care providers who meet your needs and expectations.

1. To me, the term "Quality Child Care" means:

_____

_____

_____

2. My family will benefit from quality child care in the following ways:

_____

_____

_____

3. My hopes for my child's experience in child care are:

_____

_____

_____

4. My greatest fears about placing my child in child care are:

_____

_____

_____

You have now discovered quite a mix of individual concerns and expectations about child care. Now we have the opportunity to determine how these feelings guide you in evaluating the types of child care available. Learning about the types of child care, and how to pay for it, is the subject of the next section.

Section II: Introducing the Types of Child Care and Financing

Section II Goal Statement: When you have completed this section you will gain a better understanding of the existing types of child care and the mechanisms available to help families cover the costs of child care.

You will also:

■ Learn about the various types of child care available

■ Obtain knowledge about various funding sources available to help pay for child care

■ Understand the need to develop a planned budget for child care expenses

Types of Child Care

Parents have many choices when considering what type of child care they want for their child. Listed below are descriptions of some types of child care from which you may choose. Please note that some child care options may not be available in your area.

Family Child Care

Family child care providers care for children in their home, either alone or with hired staff. Often, providers care for all ages of children—from infants through preschoolers as well as for elementary-aged children who arrive after school.

Here are reasons why some people prefer family child care:

▮ *Group size: The overall number of children in a group is typically smaller than in center-based care. Smaller group size can mean more attention is given to each child.*

▮ *Mixed ages: In many family child care settings there are children of mixed ages. Some parents prefer their child to be in a group setting that reflects a typical family structure.*

- *Continuity of care:* Provider turnover tends to be much lower than in other types of child care. Often children will remain with a family child care provider up to their entrance into school and frequently during after-school hours. Some parents want this type of continuity. In addition, some parents favor one child care provider instead of several teachers that a child may encounter in a center.

- *Setting:* The setting is much like home.

In-home Child Care

In-home care is provided in the home of the child and parent. An in-home provider may live with the family (for example, a live-in nanny or *au pair*), or live out of the home and provide care in the home during specified hours.

- Nannies may be highly trained providers. As employers, parents must pay social security and some taxes. Health insurance and other benefits such as vacation and sick days are optional. Parents often provide transportation as well.

- *Au pairs* are typically college-age individuals who come to work or go to school in the U.S. on an exchange program. In addition to salary, *au pairs* receive room and board and may not work more than 45 hours weekly.

Here are reasons why some people choose in-home child care:

- *Flexibility:* In-home care offers parents the most flexibility. Parents arrange in-home care for the exact schedule they need.

- *Additional Services:* In-home care providers may provide, at increased cost, extra services for the family such as running errands, cleaning or cooking.

- *Transportation:* In-home providers may provide transportation services for family members.

- *Setting:* In the home.

As you can see, an in-home child care provider may become a fundamental and important extension of the family.

Center Based Child Care (day care center, preschool, nursery school)

Center-based child care is provided in a facility set up specifically to care for young children. Children are typically grouped by age and are cared for by staff employed by the center.

Center-based child care can take many forms and may include one or more of the following:

For-profit centers are typically owned by an individual or corporation as a single site, a franchise, or a chain of centers. Profits earned by the center are shared with owners or stockholders.

Non-profit centers are typically incorporated as non-profit organizations and are administered by paid staff, with oversight by a board of directors. Profits earned by the organization are reinvested into the center.

Religiously-sponsored programs are connected to a church or religious organization, through an affiliation which could be limited to ownership of the child care facility, or could extend to church involvement in governance and religious instruction and practices such as praying before meals and celebration of religious holidays.

Parent cooperatives are typically governed by a parent board of directors. Parents may have a high degree of involvement in center operations (for example, assistance with policy and budget writing, staff hiring, volunteering in the classroom). Parents often have access to a great deal of parenting support, guidance and resources.

Employer-sponsored programs serve the children of company employees and are operated either at or near the work site. Centers can be operated by the employer or by a child care agency. Employers often pay for the development of sponsored centers and may cover ongoing operating costs. Some employers provide parent scholarships, sliding fee scales and other subsidies to make care affordable for most employees.

Federally funded programs serve children that meet certain criteria such as educational needs or family income level. Programs typically must meet standards or regulations established by the federal government. Examples of federally funded programs include public school early education programs, Even Start and Head Start. Programs may be located in schools, child care centers, family child care homes, and in specially designed facilities.

Here are reasons why some people choose center-based child care:

- *Same-age groups: In most centers children will spend most of their day with same-age peers and are able to form relationships and play with children their own age.*

- *Transitions to school: Friendships children establish in the center carry over into school.*

- *Educational value: Many families seek a child care center with a strong focus on learning through play. Ask a prospective center about the type of educational program they provide.*

- *Setting: A center is especially designed for children.*

Other Types of Child Care

Specialized Child Care

A few other types of specialized care, which can be provided in family child care, in-home or center settings are also available. Some of these options, listed below, may be in limited supply in this country and may be more expensive than regular child care options.

Sick Child Care Programs

These programs are designed to care for mildly ill children. Hospitals in some communities also have units staffed by nurses that are specially designed for this purpose.

Emergency/Drop-in Care Centers

These centers provide emergency care for children when a parent's regular child care arrangements fall through, due to a child's illness, center closing, family provider illness or other emergency. This service can be provided by a full-service child care center or by a small specialty center.

School-age Child Care

School-age programs provide recreational and educational activities for children between the ages of 5 and 12 during hours and days when children are not in school. Types of care can include before-school care, after-school care, programs for school holidays and summer programs. School-age programs can be located in many settings including schools, neighborhood centers, child care centers and family child-care homes.

To this point, you have learned that choosing child care is a personal activity. You have also learned that the various child care options are nearly as individual as you are. While it is positive that such variety exists, it can make your choice somewhat complex and time consuming. One other factor that can make your search a bit more complicated is how you pay for child care. This is the subject that we will cover next.

3 1833 04055 8204

Finding Dollars for Child Care

While parenting broadens one's perspective, it also stretches the budget. Paying for the costs of child care is a financial hurdle for many families.

In this next section you will understand the need to develop a budget for child care expenses. In addition, you will learn about various funding sources available to help pay for child care.

Your Family Budget

Here are a few points to consider. They will help you negotiate the costs of child care:

Develop a Family Budget

■ Developing an accurate monthly budget for all expenses will help determine how much you can afford to spend for child care.

Add in Extra Child Care Cost

■ Review your household expenses and income. Add in projected child care expenses. Think of it this way: include child care expenses in your planned monthly budget along with mortgage or rent, and basic needs such as food and utilities.

■ Ask about employer-sponsored child care benefits and other assistance that might be available.

■ Remember that your child care expenses may include fees in addition to weekly tuition. These fees may include enrollment or activity fees, and the cost of lunches and snacks. There may also be additional costs for days the program may be closed when alternate care is required. You may also incur additional expenses for extended care if your child care provider is not available certain hours of the day (such as after school) and alternative arrangements must be made.

■ The cost of child care decreases as children get older.

■ Some centers or providers may require an initial deposit as an application fee. This fee does not mean your child is enrolled or even has a spot. There might be additional fees to enroll your child in the program. Also, some centers or providers will reduce fees if they care for multiple children per family.

Trim Your Expenses

■ Look for current expenses in your budget that you can comfortably reduce or eliminate to cover child care costs.

Refer for a moment to the budget worksheet on the next page. Use the budget worksheet to help clarify your monthly budget and allowance for child care.

Smart Tips for Parents

Child care is a major expense for families with young children. Many young families feel pressured financially, spending up to a third of their income on child care.

Unlike public elementary schools, which are funded through tax dollars, revenue for most child care providers and centers comes almost entirely from tuition charged to families.

As a "people industry" the majority of a provider or center's income goes directly to staff, salaries and benefits. Therefore, centers that charge the most are able to pay the most. (This, however, does not necessarily mean that they do.)

Programs that pay more are able to attract staff with more experience and education and generally experience lower staff turnover. The American adage "you get what you pay for" can apply.

 Budget Worksheet

Child care costs are calculated, predictable expenses.
Use this worksheet to total your income and expenses.

Income	Current Monthly Income
Net Monthly Income (take home pay)	
Partner's Net Monthly Income	
Other	
Total Monthly Income	A

Expenses	Current Monthly Expense
Mortgage or Rent	
Property Tax	
Transportation: Car payment, gas, tolls, parking, transit	
Utilities: Electric, gas, oil, telephone, water	
Medical Expenses: Doctor, dentist, eye care	
Insurance: Health, car, home/renter's, life	
Credit Card Debt	
Loan Payment(s): Student loan	
Groceries, Dining Out	
Household Items	
Repairs: Home, car	
Cable	
Clothing	
Education	
Entertainment	
Membership Dues: Clubs, unions, civic groups	
Personal: Haircuts, newspapers, magazines, pets, internet service	
Vacations	
Hobbies	
Gifts and Cards	
Charitable Contributions	
Other	
Total Monthly Expenses	B

Additional Expenses Related to Child Care	Expense with Child
Medical: Doctor visits, prescriptions	
Diapering Needs: Diapers (disposable or cloth), wipes, diaper rash cream, diaper service (if needed)	
Nutritional Needs: Formula (if needed), bottles, breast pump, baby food	
Clothing: Clothes, towels, washcloths, bedding, sheets, blankets	
Equipment: Stroller, high chair, crib, changing table, car seat	
Activities: Swim lessons, soccer leagues, etc.	
Activity Supplies: Toys, books, uniforms	
CHILD CARE	
Total Monthly Child Care Expenses	C

Formula

1. Enter Total Monthly Expenses (from **B**)   _____ (B)

2. Enter Total Monthly Child Care Expenses (from **C**)   + _____ (C)

3. Add Total Monthly Expenses (**B**) and
   Total Monthly Child Care Expenses (**C**)
   This equals your total monthly expenses with a child (**D**)   = _____ (D)

4. Enter Total Monthly Income (**A**)   _____ (A)

5. Subtract Total Monthly Expenses with a Child (**D**)
   from Total Monthly Income (**A**)   - _____ (D)

6. **This total is how much extra money you have available each month.**   = _____

Helpful Tips

After you have completed your budget, if you find that you have come up short, go back to your Current Monthly Expenses and reconsider some of the following expenses. You may find that you can spend less money on some of these options.

- Dining Out
- Entertainment
- Hobbies
- Cable
- Telephone
- Memberships
- Vacations
- Gifts
- Contributions
- Second Car

Sources for Help with Child Care Costs

Here are some sources that may be available in your community to help with child care costs.

Public Funding

- Your county or municipality may offer child care funding to families that meet eligibility requirements, such as income level, special needs of the child, or family issues.

Child Care Center

- Ask prospective child care providers or center staff if they have a sliding fee scale, offer scholarships or offer other forms of financial assistance. Determine the center's family income eligibility requirements for assistance.

Employers

- Contact the human resource department and ask if your employer offers any benefits to help with child care costs. Possible options include "cafeteria style" plans or other benefit options that allow you to have child care expenses deducted from your paycheck before taxes. In addition, your employer may offer child care scholarships or other forms of assistance, such as in-house or other child care affiliations.

Educational Institutions

- If you are a student at a technical school, college or university, contact the financial aid office about loans or grants that may be available to you.

Head Start

- Head Start is a free program available to families who meet enrollment guidelines. Contact the national Head Start office or your local resource and referral agency.

Tax Credits

- Low-income families are often eligible for special tax credits. You can get the credit even if you do not owe taxes, but you must file a tax return. For help in filing your taxes, contact the Internal Revenue Service toll-free 1-800-829-3676 or visit the IRS web site: www.irs.gov

There are many ways that you can make the desirable affordable when it comes to paying for child care. In this section, we have focused on "sharpening your pencil" to help cover the costs of child care. In the next section, you will have a chance to "sharpen your focus" by defining your child care preferences.

Smart Tips for Parents

Many working parents experience feelings of guilt about leaving their baby with a child care provider. However, there is no reason for you to feel guilty. In fact, a study reported in the April 1999 issue of *Good Housekeeping* magazine finds little evidence to support the notion that families with two working parents short-change their children.

Researchers at the University of Michigan Institute for Social Research found that in so-called traditional families (father at work, mother at home), parents spent an average of 22 hours a week engaged with their children. In families where both mother and father worked, children received 19 hours of their parents' time per week.

"There is a tendency to assume that two-working-parent families are neglecting their children, but this study found little evidence of that," says Sandra Hofferth, a senior research scientist at the institute.

Defining Your Preferences: Activity #2

Getting to Know Yourself and What You Need in Child Care

Before you begin a serious search for child care it is a good idea to identify your needs and thoroughly understand your situation.

If you were suddenly asked "What type of child care do you need?" you might be at a loss in coming up with an answer. Certainly you would have some basic ideas in response to this question. You might provide answers like these:

"The providers must be warm, nurturing and well trained" or,

"The providers must have a program that my child will enjoy."

Many other factors will contribute to your personal definition of quality child care. To get you thinking about them, read the questions below. There are no correct answers to these questions. They serve only to bring clarity to your child care search.

- Do you prefer child care in your house, someone else's house or in a child care center?

- What about location? Would you like child care closer to your house, your workplace or your partner's workplace?

- Is access to public transportation routes important to you?

- Is the provider safety conscious, such as educated in first-aid and CPR?

- Is the provider a licensed provider?

- What does your budget allow for child care?

- How often do you need child care? Every day or just a few hours every now and then?

- What type of environment do you want your child to be in? Mixed ages, same ages? What about group size? How many children is your child comfortable with in a child care setting?

Remember that your preferences may change over time. Factors such as your child's age, personal values, changes in your work or family situation, and your feelings about and experiences with child care can affect the type of child care you find most appropriate.

Defining Your Preferences

Please circle the letter that best describes your preference.

A. The Basics

1. My child care should be located...
   a) Closer to my house or in my house.
   b) Closer to my workplace.
   c) Closer to my partner's workplace.
   d) Location not critical.
   e) Near public transportation routes.

2. I want to pay for my child care...
   a) As much as my budget will allow.
   b) As little as possible.

3. My schedule is....
   a) Regular. I need child care for my child on the same days for the same hours each week.
   b) Variable. I need flexibility in the days and amount of time my child will be in child care.

B. Your Specific Preferences

4. The Setting:
   a) I like the idea of my child in a home-like setting with just one provider.
   b) I like the idea of my child in a setting designed for children with many providers in the building.
   c) I like the idea of my child being cared for by a provider in my home.
   d) Not sure.

5. Age Considerations:
   a) I want my child to be in a group of children of mixed ages (with a group that could include infants, toddlers, preschool- and school-age children all together with the same provider).
   b) I want my child to be in a group of children of the same age range (all infants in one group, all toddlers in one group, all preschool-age children in another).
   c) I want my child to be cared for alone or just with his or her siblings.
   d) Not sure.

6. Group Size:
   a) I prefer a smaller-sized (less than 8 children) group of children for my child.
   b) I don't mind a slightly larger group (more than 8 children but within the state-regulated group size) of children for my child.
   c) I want one-on-one, individual care for my child.
   d) Not sure.

X+Y=? What Your Choices Mean

A. The Basics:

1. Location: If you answered "A", "B", "C" or "E" you need to consider location seriously when choosing child care. Take a map and mark a radius around your home, workplace or partner's workplace so you know which child care options will fall into your location requirement.

   If you answered "D", location will not be a major factor for you in considering your child care options.

2. Cost: If you answered "A", you probably have already set a budget and determined how much money your budget will allow you to spend on child care.

   If you answered "B", money is an issue in considering child care. You may want to rethink your budget to allow more money for child care. You may also want to check into any benefits your employer may offer for child care. Remember, some child care centers offer scholarships.

3. Schedule: If you answered "A", scheduling will not be much of an issue for you. You will not have much difficulty locating a child care provider who can meet your scheduling needs. Most child care providers prefer you to commit to a regular schedule for your child.

   If you answered "B", scheduling will be an issue as you search for child care. You will need to locate a child care provider who will accommodate your changing schedule.

B. Your Specific Preferences:

If you answered all or mostly "A" to questions 4, 5 and 6, your preferences may lead you to choose family child care as your preferred mode of child care. Family child care offers a home-like setting with usually one provider on-site, a smaller group size and a mixed-age group.

If you answered all or mostly "B", your preferences may lead you to choose center-based child care. Center-based care offers a school-like setting with more providers on site, a slightly larger group size and children are often grouped by age level.

If you answered all or mostly "C", your preferences may lead you to choose a nanny or in-home child care provider. Nannies offer a more individual one-on-one type of care in your home. Nannies often are employed to do light housekeeping duties as well as child care.

If you answered all or mostly "D", you are not sure how to answer these questions. Take time to read through this material when you get home, visit some potential providers and come back to this question again after you have gathered more ideas and information. It is okay to be "not sure" at this time. Some parents may need to look at specific programs before they are ready to make a decision.

Bringing it all together:

You may have to make conscious tradeoffs or discuss how to balance what you want with what you realistically need or can afford.

After considering location, schedule, types of programs (center vs. family vs. in-home care) and personal factors are important considerations.

■ Do you have particular personal or family values that you want represented in the child care provider you choose for your child? These values may center on issues such as religion, ethnicity and language.

■ Does your child have special needs that will require a provider to have specialized training?

By now, you have a good understanding of the types of child care, some ideas on how to budget and prepare financially and a basic definition of your child care preferences. In the next section you will learn about indicators of quality care.

Section III: What are the Indicators of "Quality Child Care"?

Section III Goal Statement: When you have completed this section, you will know the basics of child care licensing. In addition, you will understand the importance of national accreditation and adult-to-child ratios.

You will be able to:

■ Gain an overview of state child care licensing, including definitions of licensing terms

■ Become familiar with characteristics that may distinguish providers of high quality child care

■ Understand the value of accreditation

■ Learn about the type of child care that best meets your needs

■ Make better informed decisions when choosing child care

■ Clarify the distinction between "adult-to-child" ratio and "maximum group size"

■ Understand the types of licensing violations, complaints and conditions of a license

Licensing

Licensing: The Basic Level of Regulation

In the United States, there is no comprehensive national child care policy. There are few, if any, federal laws that govern the child care industry, with the exception of federally funded child care. (Example: Head Start.)

The fact is, in the child care industry, not all providers or centers offer programs of equal quality. That's why the quest for quality can sometimes be challenging.

There is a well known saying in the business world which is "caveat emptor," which means "buyer beware." Parents searching for quality child care must take great care to make sure the program they select is a good one.

The search for quality child care begins by identifying those programs which have at least a minimal level of regulation. This minimal level of regulation is determined by each state through its licensing regulations.

Licensing: What Does Licensing Cover?

Licensing rules govern the basic operation of child care centers and family child care homes. Rules are set and enforced by each state. Specific rules vary from state to state. In most states there are separate rules for family child care providers and for center-based providers.

To find the specific regulations for your state, contact The National Resource Center for Health and Safety in Child Care. Call this Center toll-free at 1-800-598-KIDS, fax 303-724-0960 or write, NRC for Health and Safety in Child Care, Campus Mail Stop F541, P.O. Box 6508, Aurora, CO 80045-0508. Visit this Center's web site at: http://nrc.uchsc.edu

Licensing rules generally fall into four basic and important categories. They are:

- Regulations about Health and Safety

- Regulations about Staffing: Group Size and Ratios

- Regulations about Discipline of Children

- Requirements for Child Care Providers

Regulations About Health and Safety

- Emergency plans, fire protection

- Sanitation: hand washing, diapering, toilet facilities and meals

- Furnishings, indoor and outdoor spaces

Health and safety are among the most important characteristics of any child care program. Regulations in this area deal with the condition of the family child care home or center. The regulations specifically list what types of safety precautions should be taken in the environment for the ages of children present. These regulations also govern health issues such as hand washing, sanitizing diaper areas and administering medications.

Staffing: Group Size and Ratios

- Adult-to-child ratios are the ratios of child care providers to children.

- Group size is the maximum number of children that can be in a room or area together.

- Maximum allowable group sizes and ratios are set based on the age of the children. In general, the younger the child, the lower the required ratios and group size.

- There is considerable state-to-state variation in required ratios and group sizes.

- When there is a mixed-age group, many states require that the maximum group size followed should be the group size indicated for the youngest children in the group. For example, let's say the maximum allowable group size for two-year olds in this state is 12. If two-year olds are in a mixed-age group with older children, the maximum allowable group size is still 12.

- What do the numbers mean? Generally, the smaller the group, the less overwhelming the experience is for the child. Lower numbers of children per provider mean potentially more individual attention for children. Look for a provider or center whose adult-to-child ratios are lower than state requirements.

Regulations About Discipline of Children

- Prohibits the use of corporal punishment. (Practices that frighten, humiliate, or harm children. Examples include spanking, shaming or isolating children, or withholding food).

- Protects children from child abuse and neglect.

Many licensing laws related to discipline are designed to prevent child abuse. Most states require child care providers to put their discipline policy in writing for parents to review. If you do not see such a policy, be certain to ask about it.

Requirements for Child Care Providers

- Minimum education or training, continuing education requirements

- Criminal background checks

Smart Tips for Parents

- Higher quality in a program may relate to lower numbers of children and higher numbers of adult care providers.

- Look for a program that has a fewer number of children-per-provider than the state standard.

- Children may receive more attention when there are lower numbers of children per adult care provider.

Many states require training in child care and development to become a child care provider. A provider who exceeds the basic state requirement may be more dedicated to the profession and more likely to continue to improve his/her skills in child care. A provider may be required to complete a set number of continuing education credits or hours yearly in topics related to child care or child development. A provider may also be required to have a criminal background check and may be ineligible to care for children if he/she has a record of crimes involving children or other serious crimes.

Understanding Licensing Violations

Parents should understand a few basic facts about the potential for centers or providers to be in violation of child care licensing rules. Parents should also understand how licensing departments deal with suspected violations. Here are some specifics:

- When a center or family child care program is inspected for its license, there may be one or more requirements (licensing rules) that are not met. If this provider is identified as being "non-compliant", the licensing department informs the center or provider in writing of all areas of non-compliance and provides time for corrections to be made.

- A complaint is an allegation that a center or provider is operating illegally or is violating one or more licensing rules. Complaints can be made anonymously and can typically be submitted to the department by telephone, letter or personal interview. Each state has its own procedure for handling complaints. Typically, a report is created, the complaint is investigated, and if the compliant is verified, some action is taken. The action taken depends on the seriousness of the violation and may include a citation with a specified time to fix the problem, a fine, or program closure.

- A licensing department may refuse to grant a license, may revoke a license, or may suspend a license of the center or provider under conditions which may include: involvement in a pending criminal charge; conviction of a crime related to the care of the child; a determination of child abuse or neglect; or a finding of imminent danger to the health, safety and welfare of the children in care.

There is another level of quality you can seek in a child care provider. It is known as accreditation.

Accreditation

A Step Beyond Licensing and Regulation

Some child care providers or centers choose to take a step beyond licensing and regulation. They seek what is known as national accreditation.

Smart Tips for Parents

Just because a center or family child care provider is not licensed does not automatically mean that it is operating illegally. Factors that may exclude licensing requirements are numbers of children served and provider fees.

Smart Tips for Parents

Every state determines the circumstances under which a center or family child care home must be licensed.

Accreditation is practiced in many settings. Colleges and universities seek accreditation of their educational programs. Hospitals seek accreditation of their patient care services. For the most part, accreditation assures a certain high level of professional standards, commitment to excellence and quality services.

Although there is no national regulation of child care, accreditation is a national certification. Accreditation is an indicator that a program has attained a level of quality that exceeds basic licensing requirements.

Through the voluntary accreditation process, providers take an in depth look at their skills and the environment, materials and activities they offer for children and families.

While it is usually true that providers and centers who have taken the extra step to achieve accreditation often offer a higher quality of care, this is not a guarantee.

Accreditation: How Is It Earned?

How does a child care provider achieve accreditation? Accredited homes and centers voluntarily exceed the minimum licensing standards to achieve national standards of quality. These standards have been established by acknowledged child care organizations.

Care providers in nationally accredited programs participate in ongoing training in child development and early childhood education. Trained providers are more likely to understand children's needs and abilities at different ages, to plan appropriate activities, and to interact with children in positive ways.

Listed below are two national accreditations. In your geographical area, there may be state or local agencies or organizations which also have quality assurance standards for child care programs and centers.

Contact the sources listed in *For More Information* on page 24 to help you search for accreditation agencies in your area. Keep this in mind: lack of an accreditation does not necessarily mean that any child care program is illegal or of poor or lesser quality.

- **National Association for the Education of Young Children (NAEYC)**
  This association accredits programs or family child care homes that exceed minimum licensing and regulation standards.

- **National Association for Family Child Care (NAFCC)**
  This association accredits family child care homes that meet the child care standards defined by state licensing and regulation agencies and that have demonstrated a commitment to reach beyond the minimum requirements to achieve professional standards of excellence. The evaluation and validation procedures involve:
  - verification of licensing/regulation

Smart Tips for Parents

Licensing is a minimal level of regulation. Accreditation is an indication that a higher level of program quality has been achieved. It is important to remember that neither licensing nor accreditation alone guarantee a program's quality.

■ observation in the family child care home

■ review of family child care records and documents

■ interviews with the family child care provider

■ provider's written report

For More Information:

■ National Association for the Education of Young Children (NAEYC)
1509 16th St., N.W.
Washington, D.C. 20036-1426
1-800-424-2460 ext 333
email: academy@naeyc.org
web site: www.naeyc.org

■ National Association for Family Child Care (NAFCC)
525 SW 5th Street, Suite A
Des Moines, IA 50309
515-282-8192
Fax: 515-282-9117
email: nafcc@nafcc.org
web site: www.nafcc.org

■ Child Care Aware
1-800-424-2246 (9 a.m.-8 p.m.)

Section IV: Finding Quality Child Care in Centers and Family-based Care

Section IV Goal Statement: When you have completed this section you will identify the steps required in searching for quality child care.

You will be able to:

■ Gain an understanding of the steps in searching for quality child care and will practice several steps in the search process

■ Learn to use the telephone "like a pro" in your initial investigations of potential child care providers or centers. In addition, you will learn the right questions to ask and how to judge the answers

■ Make good use of available resources and reference materials in searching for quality child care

■ Conduct fact-finding tours, interviews and drop-in visits

■ Understand the importance of a provider's written policies and procedures

- Better evaluate whether a center or provider will meet your family needs for child care

- Develop appropriate questions to ask prospective child care providers or centers about potential health and safety issues, their program and the child care provider(s)

- Understand the conditions that may require a quick search for child care

- Conduct a search for quality child care quickly, should the need arise

An Overview of the Search Process

Seven important steps comprise the search process:

1. Research Your Options:
   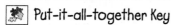 Resource List

2. Telephone Inquiry:
   Telephone Questions

3. Interview Providers and Centers:
   Interview Providers & Centers Outline

4. Take a Tour:
   What-to-look-for Guide

5. Observe the Program in Action:
   Observe the Program in Action Checklist

6. Put It All Together:
   Select the Finalists and Make Your Decision
   Put-it-all-together Key

7. Evaluate:
   Evaluation Form

Smart Tips for Parents

- Some studies indicate that families spend a minimum of five weeks searching for child care. Even after such a search, some find that the arrangements fall apart for one reason or another. Other families experience a disruption in their lives, and may go through several different child care situations before they find one that works.

- Use the tools, checklists and interview outlines in *Choosing Quality Child Care* to help make a good, long-lasting child care choice for your family.

This section provides the practical real-world information you can use to good advantage in your search.

In this section you will gain information to help you evaluate child care providers or centers that you visit. You will also practice seven steps in the search for quality child care.

Now that you know about child care regulation, understand some of the basic characteristics of quality programs and have had an opportunity to explore a variety of care options, you are ready for an introduction to the steps in the process of searching for quality care.

Before we get to the practical tips, a few words of caution:

- Following these steps cannot guarantee that you will find the "perfect" child care match.

- Barriers to finding quality care exist in every community. These barriers may include a lack of such facilities in operation, a shortage of current openings, unsuitable cost, or inconvenient location.

This seven-step process can help you identify and select the best possible child care options.

A common question many parents have is: "When do I start my search?" There is no one answer that serves all family situations.

Some parents will start as soon as they find out they are expecting; others will wait until the baby is delivered. What is right for you depends on your own circumstances. You will be the best judge of when you need to begin the search.

The time it takes to find quality child care is *as individual as you are.* That is, there is no correct length of time to spend searching for quality child care. The search will be as long as it needs to be. The best advice is to begin your search well in advance of when child care is needed.

Be forewarned, however, that infant care is the hardest to find. You should be prepared to spend some energy in this type of search. There are several reasons why quality infant care is the toughest to find, including:

- Infant care requires high adult-to-infant ratios

- It is difficult for child care centers or providers to remain profitable in infant care because of the low number of children cared for

- Infant care is demanding; babies can get sick, become fussy and often demand more of a care provider.

Step 1 Research Your Options:
Resource List

Ask friends, family and co-workers for their recommendations. Call your local child care resource and referral agency for a list of child care centers in your area. Make a list of all of the agencies you will contact and all prospective child care providers and centers. Include each phone number and address. Be willing to add providers and centers to your list as you proceed in the search.

You may want to drive past the facility before you conduct a telephone interview. Driving past may give you an idea whether you want to inquire further.

Smart Tips for Parents

- As you begin your search for child care, be sure to ask the centers or providers what their enrollment cycle is. In other words, check to see how quickly their spots fill up.

- You can learn from this parent's story:
"I thought I had eight months to find a replacement for my child care provider. I began my search in April and was interested in a pre-school setting that was to begin the following January. I quickly discovered that the pre-schools I looked into based their enrollment on the public school calendar. The providers I wanted had already completed their registrations for that fall."

Step 2 Telephone Inquiry:

📞 Telephone Questions

Use "Telephone Questions" to interview each possible provider and center. Eliminate choices that fail the interview or with whom you feel intuitively uncomfortable. A "failed interview" may occur for a number of reasons that range from lack of openings to fees that are too high, to concerns about quality. You will then be ready to schedule interviews with those that remain on the list.

Step 3 Interview Providers and Centers:

🛝 Interview Providers & Centers Outline

Set up a meeting time with the provider or center administrator when they are not responsible for caring for children. It is best to set up an appointment on the phone prior to your visit. When visiting a child care center, it is important to interview two or more teachers, if possible. This will help provide a thorough description of the program. To save time, the interview may be scheduled the same day as the tour (Step 4).

In high quality programs, center directors and providers are skilled at describing their programs and addressing parents' questions and concerns. In fact, the director or provider may answer all of your questions without having to be asked.

Use the following set of questions as a guide for your interview:

- What is your program philosophy?

- Would you describe a typical day for a child in your care?

- What is your policy on discipline?

- May I have a copy of your policies?

Step 4 Take a Tour:

🏠 What-to-look-for Guide

You should be able to tour all areas used for child care in a family child care home. You should also see all the classrooms in a center, even if your child will not be enrolled in those rooms.

Step 5 Observe the Program in Action
👓 Observe the Program in Action Checklist

Schedule an observation of the family child care program or center classroom that you are considering. An observation gives you the opportunity to see the program "in action". There are two types of visits you should make: a scheduled visit and a drop-in visit. In either situation, a brief visit will tell you a great deal about a program, and it will give you an intuitive feeling of comfort or discomfort. However, it is only a "snapshot" of the program—how it was during one period of one day, which may or may not be an accurate reflection of most days.

Factors that could affect what you see may include:

- teachers, providers or children could be nervous being "watched"

- a child could be having a bad day

- a regular classroom teacher may be absent for the day. For this reason you may want to ask the provider or center administrator if you can return for an unannounced "drop-in" visit.

Drop-in Visit

A drop-in visit should be part of every parent's planned search for quality child care. A drop-in gives you the opportunity to return to view the program during a different time, activity or day of the week. On a return visit, see if the program quality and practices are similar to those observed on your first visit.

Because a drop-in visit is unannounced, be prepared to go with the flow. You may be observing a visiting musician, spending a long morning outside on a beautiful day, or showing up to an empty facility because providers and children are enjoying a field trip.

Step 6 Put It All Together:
Select the Finalists and Make Your Decision
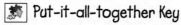 Put-it-all-together Key

This is the step where you should closely evaluate your top three choices and make a decision.

Select a provider or center and make the necessary arrangements to enroll your child. Ask about the center's "probationary period policy". This policy outlines the conditions and time frame within which the parent or program can withdraw the child without a standard advance notice. The policy also addresses the issue of fee refunds.

Step 7 Evaluate:

▣ Evaluation Form

After enrolling your child, continue to ask questions, observe and evaluate your decision. If you or your child are not happy or have doubts about your choice, do not hesitate to explore other options.

So you thought choosing quality child care would be as easy as 1-2-3. Actually, as you've just seen, it involves seven important steps, from researching your options to evaluating your selection once you have made your decision. The material we just completed is meant to give you a quick overview of the search process. Let's dig a little deeper now and proceed to The Search Process: Step 1, Research Your Options.

The Search Process:
Step 1
Research Your Options

🐾 Resource List
Activity 3

The Value of Resources and References

For the next minute or two we are going to focus on 'the two Rs' of the search for quality child care. The two Rs stand for resources and references.

- ▮ **"Resources"** provide objective information about the type and availability of child care. A resource may be an office in your community that provides information about or referrals to child care providers or centers.

- ▮ **"References"** can provide insight into a program's people and quality-of-service—from the perspective of someone who has been a "customer." In other words, this is what we sometimes refer to as "word of mouth" advertising. This type of advertising remains a valuable and trusted means of acquiring information.

The Search Process: Research Your Options

A wealth of information exists for parents seeking child care. Your challenge as a parent seeking quality child care is to make the best use of the information and time available to you in your search for quality care.

You can obtain information from a variety of sources including:

- ■ family, relatives and friends

- ■ resource and referral agencies

- ■ religious communities and community centers

The Value of Personal References

Friends, relatives and co-workers can be valuable sources in recommending (or not recommending) centers and providers. These people are valuable to you because they may share some of your preferences, values, needs and wants. So-called "word of mouth" advertising is especially valuable in a search as important as quality child care.

You should be aware of one particular consideration when it comes to judging personal references. Because such references are based on opinions, they may not be as objective as other sources. Be sure to evaluate the center or provider yourself before making a final decision.

Here are some good questions to ask people in your personal network:

- What did you like (or dislike) about the center or provider?

- How did your child enjoy the child care experience?

- How did the provider or center respond to you as a parent?

- Was the provider or center respectful of your values and culture?

- Would you recommend the provider or center?

- If your child is no longer with the provider or center, why did you leave?

Resource and Referral Agencies

Many agencies exist to provide parents with tips on how to locate and select quality child care. You can contact agencies in your area and receive referrals to regulated child care providers or centers. Remember that such referrals are restricted to those listed with the referral agency and that the agency may or may not have information about program quality.

Here are some good questions to ask people who staff the agency phone:

- What regulations should child care providers meet in my area?

- Is there a record of complaints about the provider or center I am considering?

- How do I find out about such complaints?

Community Sources of Information

- Yellow pages and business pages of the telephone book
  - provide a general list of child care options in your area

  - are limited to centers and care providers listed in the telephone book

  - are helpful in eliminating child care options by location

  - do not provide information on quality

- Advertisements
  - provide general information about centers or care providers

- are limited to those that choose to advertise
- do not provide information on quality
- The Internet
  - provides a list of local, national or global child care options
  - does not give information on quality
  - provides, through links to related sites, information related to child development and parenting (consider www.careguide.net).

Child Care Aware

To locate a resource and referral agency in your area and your state licensing office, contact Child Care Aware. Call toll-free 1-800-424-2246.

Accreditation Sources

For a listing of all accredited day care centers and family child care homes, contact:

- National Association for the Education of Young Children (NAEYC)
  1509 16th St., N.W.
  Washington, D.C. 20036-1426
  1-800-424-2460 ext 333
  email: academy@naeyc.org
  web site: www.naeyc.org

- National Association for Family Child Care (NAFCC)
  525 SW 5th Street, Suite A
  Des Moines, IA 50309
  515-282-8192
  Fax: 515-282-9117
  email: nafcc@nafcc.org
  web site: www.nafcc.org

A Resource Tool for You

A handy Resource List is included on the next page. It will help you in two ways:

- One, to list agencies, facilities or providers you wish to contact;
- Two, to write down the names of individuals who can provide you with further information or ideas.

Think of the list you just created as your 'action plan' to collect more information about potential child care providers or centers. The people or agencies you have identified should help you a great deal.

Smart Tips for Parents

There is good news and bad news about child care information via the Internet. The good news: the volume of information is substantial. The bad news: you must take a "reader beware" approach to the content. In addition, for any site that lists child care choices, be sure to consider the content a list and not a recommendation. The following web sites may help you acquire information.

General Child Development Web Sites

www.acf.dhhs.gov
Official web sites of the US Department of Health and Human Services Administration for Children and Families

The site contains information on child support, child welfare and Head Start (a national program which provides comprehensive development services for America's low income, pre-school children ages three to five and social services for their families.)

www.careguide.net
This web site contains articles and resources on finding child-care. It contains some listings of child-care providers by city and state.

Sites Related to Child Care and Early Childhood Curriculum

www.highscope.org
Official web site of the High/Scope Educational Research Foundation

www.montessori.org
Official web site of the Montessori Foundation. It contains an electronic library and resource center.

www.awsna.org
The official web site of the Association of Waldorf Schools of North America

www.ericeece.org/reggio.html
Information and resources related to the Reggio early childhood education approach. The site also contains links to other organizations involved with the Reggio approach.

Sites Related to Child Care Resource and Referral Agencies

www.naccrra.net
Official web site of the National Association of Child Care Resource and Referral Agencies

To uncover your own favorite sites on the world wide web, visit one of the web's search engines and type in a key word and then click the "search" key. Here are some commonly used search engines:

www.yahoo.com
www.excite.com
www.google.com
www.infoseek.com
Applicable key words may include: child care, children, early childhood education, highscope, montessori, reggio, and child development.

Research Your Options

Resource List
for Choosing Quality Child Care

Section IV
Search Process
Step 1, Activity 3

Date	Name		Phone	Comments
	Address		Contact	

Date	Name		Phone	Comments
	Address		Contact	

Date	Name		Phone	Comments
	Address		Contact	

Date	Name		Phone	Comments
	Address		Contact	

Date	Name		Phone	Comments
	Address		Contact	

Date	Name		Phone	Comments
	Address		Contact	

Date	Name		Phone	Comments
	Address		Contact	

Date	Name		Phone	Comments
	Address		Contact	

Date	Name		Phone	Comments
	Address		Contact	

We are now going to turn our attention to the telephone inquiry—a vital resource when it is used correctly.

The Search Process:
Step 2
Telephone Inquiry

 Telephone Questions

How to Use the Telephone Like a Pro

If you are like many parents, the telephone will be a primary resource in gathering information in your search. Telephone screening offers the advantages of convenient and quick evaluation. It should not, however, take the place of a personal visit.

Have you ever received a call from a telemarketer? If you have, you probably have an idea of how well prepared their presentation is. You should be prepared in the same way when you conduct your initial evaluations of potential child care providers or centers.

There were two important words in the paragraph you just read: initial evaluations. You can best use the telephone interview to help you narrow the list of prospective providers and centers. You do this by learning the right questions to ask and how to judge the answers you receive.

Included in this guide is a telephone interview tool for your use. Use it as a guide every time you speak to a potential child care provider or center.

Smart Tips for Parents

- The telephone is a valuable tool in gathering initial information about child care providers or centers.

- A telephone interview should never substitute for a personal visit to a prospective child care provider or center.

- When conducting a telephone interview parents should be sure to ask about "projected openings" as well as "current openings."

- When calling an in-home care provider, parents should be aware that their call may take the care provider away from the children. You may need to schedule a call at a convenient time, such as during naps.

Telephone Questions

American Red Cross

Name of provider: _____

Use the questions below to guide your interview with providers or center administrators.
The hints are only to guide you and provide further insight.

Questions	Answers you receive
Begin your conversation by supplying the age of your child and the care schedule you are seeking.	
1. Do you have an opening for my child? Do you have any projected openings? *Hint: If the answer is "no", you do not need to proceed with this center or provider.*	
2. What are the hours and days of operation? *Hint: Is the program open early and late enough to meet your needs? If not, can you arrange for someone else to drop off or pick up your child? If both answers are "no" you do not need to proceed.*	
3. Where are you located? *Hint: Determine if the distance from your home or work site is reasonable? Factor in transportation schedules and routes if you take public transportation. If the answer is "no", you do not need to proceed.*	
Note: If the answers for 1-3 are satisfactory and time is limited you may wish to ask if written program information is available. You may review the material at a later time.	
4. What is the daily or weekly rate or cost for my child's schedule? *Hint: Determine whether you can afford the tuition.*	
5. What additional fees do you charge? *Hint: Be sure to include in your estimate additional fees charged by the program. Who provides meals or snacks? Who supplies diapers?*	
6. How many days per year is the program closed? *Hint: It is typical and reasonable for high quality programs to close for major holidays.* Do you charge for closed days? *Hint: Many family child care (FCC) programs will also close for provider vacations and sick days. Closed days might mean that you pay twice: for child care you do not receive and for alternate care. You must determine what you can afford.*	
7. Is financial assistance available? *Hint: If tuition costs are too high and no assistance is available, you do not need to proceed.*	
8. Are you licensed, accredited or possess other certifications? *Hint: This is a an important issue. The center or provider may not be required to be licensed in your state.*	

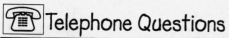
Questions	Answers you receive
9. How many children are in your care? *Hint: Large group size or few adults per child translates into less individual attention and supervision per child.* What are the ages of children in your care? *Hint: For center-based providers, ask about adult-to-child ratio and group sizes in your child's age group.*	
10. For family child care: What is your educational background and training? *Hint: Little or no training in child care and development can signal poor quality care.* For centers: How many of your teachers have 2-year or 4-year degrees? *Hint: Programs with staff that exceed minimal licensing requirements for training and education are more likely to provide high quality care.*	
11. For family child care: How long have you been providing care? *Hint: In the child care industry turnover is higher than in many fields.* For centers: How many teachers have been with you more than one year? More than 5, 10? *Hint: Turnover tends to be highest in programs where wages are lowest and working conditions are poorest. High turnover interrupts care and child and staff bonding, and produces stress on staff.*	
12. Do you serve children with special needs? What kinds of specialized training do you (FCC) or staff (center) have to serve the special social, emotional or learning needs children? *Hint: These are important questions if your child has special physical challenges that require special staff training and more individual attention for the child.*	
13. Do you provide transportation? *Hint: This is important if you require help with transportation.*	
14. When can I make an appointment to visit? *Hint: If the provider or administrator is unwilling to allow you to visit and observe it may be a better option to consider other providers or centers.*	
15. Do you have any hand-outs or other written program materials that you would be willing to send me? *Hint: A review of these materials will confirm and validate information from your interview.*	
Write your own individual questions here:	

Telephone Questions

Many parents begin their quest for quality child care via the telephone. With the right questions in hand, the telephone can give you the information you need to narrow the list of prospective providers and centers—quickly and conveniently.

The telephone can also save you the frustration of pursuing child care options that are not practical or desirable for you due to such factors as cost, location, hours or questionable quality.

Think of any other questions you can ask as well. There is additional space at the bottom of the page to write in your own questions.

After Your Telephone Inquiry

At the end of each call, determine whether you wish to keep or remove the provider or center from your list of prospective programs. You will then be ready to begin your visits and observations.

Be sure to use a new Telephone Questions page for each provider or center you are investigating. Extra copies of this telephone interview may be found in the back of the Search Guide.

The Search Process: Step 3 Interview Providers and Centers

 Interview Providers & Centers Outline

A personal visit with a prospective child care center or provider helps you develop an "intuitive" feel for the program and how your child will fit. The purpose of this visit is for you to ask more indepth questions than those that were asked during the telephone inquiry.

You should be prepared with certain key questions to ask of child care providers, teachers or center administrators. Here are some key things to think about as you plan your face-to-face visit:

- Following your telephone inquiry, call programs you wish to visit and set up a time to personally meet with care providers, teachers or center administrators.

- Keep in mind that the personal interview may be scheduled on the same day that you take a tour of the facility or family child care home.

- Use the "Interview Providers and Centers Outline" as a guide. It includes questions that are important at this stage of your search.

Smart Tips for Parents

■ Policies and procedures are important for parents because they let them know what is expected of them as parents, and policies and procedures let parents know what they can expect from the center. Policies and procedures help shape and give life to the program. Look for them in any program you are seriously considering.

- The questions in this Outline are detailed and thorough. Many high quality programs are familiar with providing answers to questions such as these. In fact, they may even answer many of these questions before you have a chance to ask them.

- You may have your own questions as well. Use the blank spaces in the Outline to write in your own questions before you visit a prospective child care center or family child care home.

- Be sure to ask if you can talk to other parents who have children cared for in this setting.

- When you return home from your personal visit, review the information you have collected. Be sure to complete such a review after each prospective provider you visit.

 # Interview Providers & Centers Outline

Name of provider: _____

Questions	Answers	Other Information
1. What is your program philosophy? 💡 *Hint: A sound philosophy will help clarify the provider's approach to child care.*		
2. Describe a typical day for a child in your care. (Ask for a copy of the daily schedule.) 💡 *Hint: The program should have a basic daily schedule. Play time should occur in large blocks (at least an hour) during the day.*		
3. What is your policy on discipline? 💡 *Hint: A quality program should not use practices that frighten, humiliate or harm children (examples include spanking, shaming or isolating children or withholding food). Make sure that your child care provider will **never** shake your baby or hit or physically abuse your child. These practices are forbidden by licensing rules in many states.*		
4. How many teachers will each group of children have in a day? Is there a primary lead teacher? Generally, what is the education, training and experience of the care providers? 💡 *Hint: Numbers of teachers or providers per numbers of children is important. Training and experience of care providers is equally important and indicates commitment and professional achievement.*		
5. How many snacks or meals are included? What kinds of foods are provided? Are monthly or weekly menus posted or provided to parents? 💡 *Hint: Meals and nutrition are important for growing children. A good program will have ready answers to these questions.*		
6. What forms need to be filled out and on file? What deposits must be made? Is there a contract to sign? Is there a trial period when starting? How long? 💡 *Hint: Enrollment policies and procedures are important in getting your child into the program.*		

Questions	Answers	Other Information
7. Ask for a set of written policies and a parent handbook. See page 39 for a checklist to review policies at home. Hint: Centers should have written policies. They should be willing to give these documents to you. You should ask about: —withdrawal policies and how much notice needs to be given —late pick-up fees —how the center or provider deals with parent and center/provider vacation days, and —how the center or provider deals with sick children		
8. What are your hours of operation? Hint: Are the hours compatible with your work schedule? How flexible is the provider's schedule? That is, will the provider allow early or late pick-us and drop-offs for special circumstances?		
9. Why should I choose your program?		
10. What distinguishes your program from others?		
11. Additional questions you may have.		

The following are policies that a center or provider should have. Use these questions to review the policies after you return home.

Goals and Philosophy
What are the goals and philosophies of the provider or the center?

Hours or Days of Operation
What days is the center closed (holidays, school vacations, provider sick days or vacations)? Do we pay for those days? Are there any late pick-up fees or early drop-off fees?

Financial Policies
On what days are payments or tuition due? Are extra fees imposed if payment is late? Is scholarship or tuition assistance available?

Enrollment Policies
What forms need to be filled out and on file? What deposits must be made? Is there a contract to sign? Is there a trial period when starting? How long?

Withdrawal Policies
How much notice (by parents or care providers) needs to be given for withdrawal? What is the center's refund policy?

Education Policies
What types of educational activities are offered for children? Is a particular curricula or educational approach used in the program?

Staff-to-child Interactions
How many teachers will each group of children have in a day? Is there a primary lead teacher? Generally, what is the education, training and experience of the care providers?

Meals and Nutrition
How many snacks or meals are included? What kinds of foods are provided? Are monthly or weekly menus posted or provided to parents?

Health and Safety
What are the center's policies related to health: such as illness, sanitation, medications and emergency plans regarding fire escape routes and tornado drills? What are the center's policies related to childrens' safety: such as treatment of injuries, release of children, activities away from the center, use of car seats and restraints? Does the center have liability insurance? Does the center have automobile insurance?

Discipline
What types of discipline are used? What types of discipline are prohibited?

Parental Involvement

What is the center's policy on confidentiality of information regarding my family and child? Does the center have an open-door policy? How is information shared about my child and how he or she is doing in the program? Are there opportunities or requirements for parental involvement that I should know about? Does the center have any appeal policies regarding administrative decisions? Do parents evaluate the quality of the program? How often?

There is no denying the fact that policies and procedures provide a solid foundation for a prospective child care provider or center. The next step you can take will be a tour of the facility.

The Search Process: Step 4 Take a Tour

 What-to-look-for Guide

Making the Most of a Tour

A tour is a method to acquire an overview of the program and facility. On a tour, you will:

- usually be with a staff person or the provider

- often be engaged in conversation throughout the tour

- move through the entire facility

- be able to see locations in which children are cared for and where they play.

In an observation, which is covered in the next section, you will:

- likely observe the setting on your own

- be in one location for a set period of time

- only be able to observe certain parts of the center or provider's program of care due to time constraints.

You should be prepared for a variety of types of tours. That is, some tours may offer just a superficial view of facility layout and design while other tours may be more comprehensive in nature.

Some tours will allow you to observe the sequence and scope of the program for a variety of ages of children.

Review the guide on the next page for some of the details to observe on your tours.

At the end of the tour, pick up an application or registration form if you think you might be interested in this program.

Remember that sometimes an application form requires a fee when it is submitted. This fee may, or may not be refundable. You should ask what the "application" means. That is, does the application guarantee a spot with this provider, or, does it just put you on a waiting list?

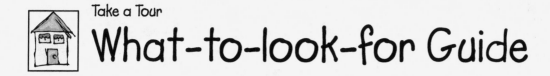

What-to-look-for Guide

American Red Cross

Name of provider: _____

What-to-look-for	Observations
The Place	
■ The environment and materials are clean, safe and in good repair.	
■ The playground is safe and protected from the street. The play area has a thick layer of wood chips or sand underneath. Play structures are not rusted, broken or have exposed areas. Play equipment is secured to the ground and is age-appropriate.	
■ All hazardous materials are stored away from children; poisons, medication, cleaning fluids, matches, sharp tools.	
■ Children are well supervised. They are within the teacher's or provider's sight and sound at all times; ratios and group sizes are at or below state maximums.	
■ Materials are stored where children can reach them: in bins and baskets or on low shelves. Furniture and equipment is child sized.	
The Program	
■ There is a regular daily schedule. Ask for a written copy.	
■ Time is provided every day for outside and inside play; physical activity and quiet play; activities that adults plan; a long period of free play. Meals, snacks and naps (in full day programs can be included). For toddlers and infants, diapering, feeding, and sleeping occur on each child's individual schedule.	
■ Materials are ample and varied. Books; art materials; climbing and riding toys; small and large blocks; dress-up clothes; dolls for pretend play; instruments and music.	
The Provider	
Relationships between adults and children	
■ Adults are warm, friendly and caring with children. Adults regard children as special and provide plenty of smiles and hugs.	
■ Discipline methods are positive and respectful. There is no corporal punishment or any type of frightening or humiliating punishment.	
■ Adults play with children during free play times, sit and talk with them during planned activities and meal times.	

As you can see, the tour offers you a basic introduction to facility layout and design. The heart and soul of the program or center deals with what you can learn by observing the program in action. Let's move to this section now.

The Search Process:
Step 5
Observe the Program in Action
 Observe the Program in Action Checklist
Activity 4

The Value of Observation
Observation is an important part of your overall search. Through observation, you can see first-hand all the elements of quality child care at work: the place, the program and the provider.

Characteristics of the "program" cover such areas as philosophy, policies and activities.

The "place" refers to issues such as health and safety, environment and equipment.

The "provider" deals with the education, experience and relationships with children and adults.

Included on the following pages is a Checklist designed to help you during the observation step. The checklist has been broken down into three sections—the place, the program and the provider—to help you focus on the elements of quality child care.

The Place
The finest child care really offers the best of two worlds: a loving, nurturing, safe and healthy environment, and personal reassurance that you have made a quality decision. But how can you be sure?

Health and safety are some of the most important issues. They are often the issues of greatest concern to parents. You can gain a good measure of assurance through careful attention to detail and using good observational skills.

The Type of Program
The child care program is also of great importance to many parents. Perhaps you favor a program with a strong focus on music, art, or educational field trips. Use this part of the Checklist to evaluate a prospective provider or center's program.

Smart Tips for Parents
- By using good observational skills and attention to detail, parents can learn a great deal about a prospective provider when they visit.

- Providers are the key to quality child care. This is the person with whom the child will spend his or her day. Providers will have a significant impact on the child's development.

- What qualities does a quality child care provider possess? What should parents look for in a teacher or provider? A provider's level of education, experience, and expertise, provides a measuring stick.

- Health and safety concerns of a child care provider or center are among the most important issues that parents consider.

The Child Care Provider

A child care provider's education, experience and expertise form the cornerstone of his or her value. Your child's teacher or provider should also be reliable, trustworthy and someone with whom you all feel comfortable.

What qualities does a quality child care provider possess? What should you look for in a teacher or provider? Use the checklist included to evaluate prospective child care teachers and providers.

You can use this checklist to evaluate all prospective providers. Although there are some traits important for all child care settings, you may feel that some qualities are more important than others.

Thoroughly read this Checklist prior to visiting any center. Remain objective throughout the process of searching for quality child care. At this point, you should consider each provider equally.

Be sure to write down your responses as you observe, or immediately after leaving the center. This will help you recall the setting much better and takes advantage of the freshness of the experience.

Use a new Checklist for each program or provider you visit. Extra copies of the Checklist are available in your Participant's Guide.

Wise use of resources and references, questions, observations and checklists will be invaluable in your search. An additional step to add to every search is the "drop-in visit."

Drop-in Visit

A drop-in visit should be part of your search for quality child care. In a drop-in visit, you have a chance to view the program of care as it exists at a specific point in time.

Because a drop-in visit is unannounced, be prepared to go with the flow. You may be observing a visiting musician, spending a long morning outside on a beautiful day, or showing up to an empty facility because providers and children are enjoying a field trip.

Once you have completed a comprehensive search process, including a drop-in visit, you are ready to put it all together and select your finalists. This is the subject of the next step.

Current information on recalled products is available at the CPSC at www.cpsc.gov or call toll-free 1-800-638-2772.

👓 Observe the Program
in Action Checklist

American Red Cross

Section IV
Search Process
Step 5, Activity #4

Name of provider: _____

What You Want To See	☺	☹	What You Don't Want To See
The Place			
■ If the center or child care home is required to be licensed, the license is posted. There are no licensing violations.			■ The center or home is required to be licensed and the license has lapsed. There are outstanding licensing violations.
■ The environment is clean, safe and in good repair. Outlets are covered; stairways are inaccessible to infants and toddlers; drapery and blind cords are out of children's reach; no chipped or peeling paint; poisonous plants are out of children's reach; and areas have adequate light, heat, and ventilation.			■ Children's areas are dirty, or look unsafe. Some or all of the items listed to the left appear unsafe.
■ Toys and equipment are clean, safe and in good repair. Toys designed for older children (with small pieces) are kept out of reach of infants and toddlers; no toys or equipment have cracked, broken, missing parts, chipped or peeling paint, or sharp edges; toys that have been in children's mouths are set aside and sanitized when children are finished with them.			■ Some or all of the toys and equipment are dirty or in poor condition. Some, or all of the items listed to the left apply to these toys and equipment.
■ In the outside play area, play spaces are separate from walkways; play spaces are separated from bodies of water (preferably by fence, which is required in some states); cushioning is provided under climbing equipment (i.e., pea gravel, wood chips); the sandbox is covered; play spaces are protected from the sun.			■ There is no outside play area, or the area is unsafe. Some or all of the items listed to the left appear unsafe.
■ All hazardous materials are stored away from children; poisons, medication, cleaning fluids, matches, sharp tools.			■ Any hazardous material is found in an area used by children.
■ Age-appropriate safety restraints are used when transporting children (car seats, seat belts).			■ Proper restraints are not used for all children or are not used at all.
■ Sleeping areas are appropriate. Cribs or playpens are provided for infants.			■ Sleeping areas are in adult beds with blankets, quilts and pillows.
■ To reduce the risk of sudden infant death syndrome (SIDS), infants should be put to sleep on their backs.			■ Infants are put to sleep on their stomachs, or care providers are indifferent when it comes to positioning prior to sleep.

What You Want To See	😊	☹	What You Don't Want To See
■ Emergency routes and plans are posted in obvious locations in each room used by children. Fire and tornado drills are practiced regularly.			■ Emergency routes and plans are a mystery; they are not posted in each room used by children. Drills are practiced occasionally or not at all.
■ Emergency numbers for fire, police and poison control are posted next to each phone. Note that not all communities have 911 service.			■ Emergency numbers are not posted, or are not by each phone.
■ Staff and children wash hands before and after eating and before preparing meals, after using the bathroom and after nose blowing. The hand washing area contains plenty of soap and disposable towels or individual cloth towels.			■ Hand washing occurs occasionally or not at all. Hand washing areas run out of supplies. Cloth towels are shared by children and staff.
■ Diaper changing practices. Adults wash hands before and after; soiled diapers are placed in a covered, foot-operated container; diapering surfaces and potty chairs are cleaned and sanitized after each use.			■ Proper diaper changing practices are not followed or are followed inconsistently.
■ Smoking does not occur in areas used by children or in children's presence.			■ Staff are seen smoking in the building, or on-site. Areas used by children smell of cigarette smoke.
■ The classroom or home is clean, attractive and inviting.			■ Classroom or home is dirty or unkempt or may contain unpleasant odors. Note that messes from active play are okay and should not be considered inappropriate.
■ Children have room to play and move around without interfering with each other.			■ The room is crowded. It is either too small or is filled with too much furniture.
■ In centers infant rooms are arranged in areas for eating, sleeping and playing. Toddler, preschool and school-age classrooms also contain areas for art, pretend play, blocks and building, fine motor play and books.			■ No clear areas are visible, or spaces are provided for some, but not all, activities listed to the left.
■ Active and quiet areas are located in different parts of the room or home.			■ Active and quiet play occurs together. The classroom is loud and chaotic with no quiet, protected places for children to be.
■ Children's art work is displayed on the walls. Wall displays are at children's eye levels.			■ Walls are bare or contain only "teacher materials" such as the alphabet, charts, colors. Wall displays are located at adult's eye levels.
■ Materials are stored where children can reach them: in bins and baskets or on low shelves.			■ Materials are stored on closed shelves or on high shelves out of children's reach. Children have to ask for what they want.

What You Want To See	☺	☹	What You Don't Want To See
■ Furniture and equipment is child-sized.			■ Furniture and equipment are too big or too small.
■ Walking children can reach toilets, sinks, changing table and other essential areas on their own (with foot stools when needed).			■ Adults have to place children on toilets. Adults wash children's hands.
The Program			
■ Children are well supervised. They are within the teacher's or provider's sight and sound at all times; ratios and group sizes are at or below state maximums; all people present during the hours of child care have a completed criminal background check; at least one teacher or provider has completed training in handling emergencies (accidents, injuries, fire, tornado); in centers, an adult is available to replace a teacher who is out of the classroom (on break, etc.) Family providers have adults to call on in emergencies.			■ Adults are "clustered" in one area, or are busy with other tasks when children are playing. Any or all of the items listed to the left seem to be apparent.
■ There is a regular daily schedule. Ask for a written copy. Activities happen in the same order each day.			■ There is no regular schedule. Children are not familiar with the schedule and order of activities. The schedule may not be available in written form.
■ Time is provided every day for outside and inside play; physical activity and quiet play; activities that adults plan; a long period of free play when children choose what to do (1 hour or more is good); time for meals, snacks and naps (in full day programs).			■ The activities listed at left do not occur or do not occur every day.
■ For young toddlers and infants, diapering, feeding, and sleeping occur on each child's individual schedule.			■ There is too much adult control, with children in large adult-controlled "lecture groups" for much of the day, or the program looks chaotic: children wander around looking bored with nothing to do, or they run around in groups.
■ Materials and activities are geared to the range of children's skill levels and interests.			■ Materials are for much younger or older children. Children seem bored with the toys.
■ Materials are available during free play times for language (books, story tapes); physical play (riding toys, equipment for climbing); textures (sand, water, modeling clay); fine motor skills (small blocks, puzzles); music (tapes/CDs, instruments). For older children materials are available for art (crayons, markers, scissors, paper); pretend play (dolls, play furniture, dress-up clothes); blocks and building (large wooden blocks, cars and trucks, boards).			■ The classroom or program has few materials or has a lot of one kind of material (blocks) but few or none of another. There may be only one of a very popular toy causing fights or issues with sharing.

What You Want To See	☺	☹	What You Don't Want To See
■ Occasional trips are taken in the neighborhood and community, such as to visit parks, museums, businesses, libraries.			■ The classroom or program does not take field trips. A television is used too frequently as an electronic babysitter.
■ Children have opportunities for learning about differences between people, how to get along together and how to solve problems and conflicts.			■ Differences between people are not discussed. Conflicts and problems are avoided or solved by teachers only.
■ Children with special needs receive the care and attention they require.			■ Children with special needs are segregated from the group, isolated or ignored.
The Provider.			
■ Teachers and providers are trained in child development, child care and education.			■ Teachers and providers have little or no formal training.
■ Teachers and providers have experience working with children in an age group for which child care is being sought.			■ Teachers and providers have little or no experience in child care or with the age group for which they provide care.
■ Teachers and providers have good references.			■ Teachers and providers are unwilling to share references or have negative references.
Relationships between adults and children			
■ Adults are warm, friendly and caring with children. Adults regard children as special and provide plenty of smiles and hugs. Staff give children individual attention while aware of needs of the whole group.			■ Adults do not seem to enjoy being with children. Adults ignore or avoid children, or seem generally angry or frustrated with children. Adults are with one child and "forget" the rest of the group.
■ Adults discipline children using words, tone of voice and gestures that are calm, respectful and positive. Note that licensing rules in many states prohibit corporal punishment and any type of frightening or humiliating punishment.			■ Adults yell at, shame or criticize children, use loud voices, use quick or rough gestures such as pulling or pushing. Adults use punishments such as isolating children in a room, threatening or spanking them.
■ Adults speak and listen to children and get down to children's eye levels.			■ Adults do not stop what they are doing to listen to children. Instead, they keep working, walking or talking with others. Adults stand when conversing with children.
■ Adults encourage children to express all feelings. Children are encouraged to express strong feelings safely, without hurting others.			■ Adults do most things for children, or give so much independence that children become frustrated.
■ Adults play with children during free play times. Adults sit and talk with children during planned activities and meal times.			■ Adults play with children only occasionally or not at all, or, supervising play from a distance or completing cleaning or other tasks.

What You Want To See	🙂	🙁	What You Don't Want To See
■ Children seem to like the teacher or provider and feel comfortable going to them to talk, play or get help.			■ Children appear nervous or uncomfortable. They may avoid contact with the teacher or provider.
Relationships between adults			
■ Teachers and providers are friendly and professional with co-workers and parents. They are sensitive to individual needs and differences.			■ Teachers and providers ignore or avoid parents or co-workers. There is tension or arguing between staff.
■ Teachers and providers share information with parents about their child and his or her activities. They answer parent questions and concerns. Parent conferences occur regularly, once or twice yearly.			■ Parents do not receive regular information about the child or his or her activities. Staff are unavailable or unwilling to answer questions. Conferences are held rarely or not at all.
■ Parents are always welcome to visit. They are encouraged to become involved in the center.			■ Parents are unable or are discouraged from visiting and helping in the class or program.
■ Parents feel comfortable in the center or home. It is the kind of place you would enjoy spending your day.			■ Parents feel uncomfortable, uneasy or unwelcome.

The Search Process:
Step 6
Put It All Together:
Select the Finalists and Make Your Decision

🧩 Put-it-all-together Key

The Value of "Homework" Rather than "Guesswork"

A thorough, well-planned search process allows you to apply "homework" rather than "guesswork" in your search for quality child care.

Doing your "homework": using resources and references, taking tours and applying observational skills will help you select a child care provider of good value.

Included on the next page is the "Put-it-all-together Key". This key will help you, in a systematic manner, evaluate your top three finalists.

Even with the help of a tool such as the "Put-it-all-together Key", some parents find decision making to be among the most difficult of tasks. Here are some helpful points:

- If you have trouble reaching a decision, visit the facility at a pick-up time and ask another parent questions about the facility and provider. Good questions to ask fellow parents may include:
  ▌ What do you like about this provider?

  ▌ What don't you like?

  ▌ Why did you choose this provider?

  ▌ Are you committed to keeping your child here? Why or why not?

- If you are unable to make a decision, you can always start the process over again if time permits.

- If your time is extremely limited, you should select the best of the finalists. You always have the option of continuing to do your homework on other providers.

Smart Tips for Parents

- Imagine yourself dropping your child off at a prospective child care provider and driving or walking away. How would you feel about leaving your child behind with this particular provider?

- It is important to evaluate all of your prospective providers in a consistent manner.

- Making the final decision and enrolling a child is often a tough decision for parents. Even though they may feel they have completed a thorough search, many parents still have some element of fear. Parents must trust their instincts about a particular provider or center.

Put-it-all-together Key

Rate your top three candidates in the following categories.
Assign a number from 1 (poor) to 5 (outstanding) to each issue,
then add your numbers down for a final score.

Category	Name of Center or Provider	Name of Center or Provider	Name of Center or Provider
The Place			
Health and Safety			
Play Area: Inside			
Outside			
Appropriate Toys and Furniture			
Environment: Active Areas			
Quiet Areas			
The Program			
Activities: Fun and Interactive			
Daily Schedule			
Ratios and Group Size			
Art, Music, Sports, Field Trips, etc.			
The Provider			
Experience			
Education			
References			
Relationships: With Adults			
With Children			
Other			
Hours			
Weekly/Monthly Cost*	/	/	/
Meal Plan			
Additional Cost*			
Location			
Score			
*Please refer to back side of sheet			

$ Dollars and Sense

Record actual dollar amounts for each option. After you have totaled weekly/monthly cost and additional cost, rate each option. Rate using a number from 1 (poor) to 5 (outstanding).

Factor	Option 1: Hours:		Option 2: Hours:		Option 3: Hours:	
	Weekly	Monthly	Weekly	Monthly	Weekly	Monthly
Regular Tuition						
Extended Care						
Activity Fee						
Meal/Snacks Fee						
Other_____ _____ _____ _____						
Total Weekly/Monthly Cost						
Rate each option on weekly/monthly cost**						
Application Fee:						
Registration Fee:						
Closed Dates: Total number of closed dates that you are charged for, or must pay for: Additional cost to cover alternative child care may need to be considered during these times.						
Total Additional Cost						
Rate each item on additional cost**						

** Copy this rating to front side of sheet.

Applications and Enrollments

A necessary step in the process is enrollment. From center to center, enrollment can mean many things.

- Is it merely completing an application?

- Are fees involved?

- Are they refundable?

- If a parent completes an application, does this guarantee a "spot" in the program or is the child on a waiting list?

Enrolling a child in a child care program often requires a good deal of paperwork including health forms, child profile information, family information and who to call in case of emergencies. In addition, many providers have an actual registration form that parents must fill out.

Some providers may require fees for a child to be placed on a waiting list. Additional fees may also be required such as those for registration. At enrollment time, down payment may also be required.

You must verify with providers, and clearly understand yourself, what the application and enrollment process means.

Many parents experience a sense of relief once the search and selection process is over. Your work doesn't end there. Ongoing evaluation is important in assessing your child care choice.

Smart Tips for Parents

Ask the child care provider how you can make the transition into child care easier on your child.

The Search Process: Step 7 Evaluate

 Evaluation Form

Every Child Deserves the Best

It is said that every child deserves the best. How do you determine that your child receives what he or she deserves?

You can gain valuable understanding of a child care provider's value to your family through "observational evaluation". Such an evaluation considers three main areas: your child, the child care provider, and yourself. Use the questions or comments below to help guide your evaluation.

Listen to Your Child:

- If your child is old enough to speak, does he or she speak in positive terms about the child care experience?

- Does your child have fun at child care or with the provider?

- Does he or she look forward to going?

- Does your child look excited and happy to see the child care provider?

Listen to Your Child Care Provider:

- Do they tell you how your child is doing or, do they remain silent?

- Are there ample opportunities for you to talk to your child care provider?

- Listen to how your child care provider describes children or the day's events.

Listen to Yourself:

- What does your gut say?

- Do you feel "right" with your child here?

- Do you feel listened to as a parent?

The answers to these important questions come through evaluation and ongoing communication with your child care provider. Consider the following important points as well:

- You should not be afraid to change your mind once you have made a decision.

- Continue with unannounced "drop-in" visits. Such visits allow a real-world view of the program at a specific point in time.

- If your child is old enough to discuss his or her opinions of the provider, be sure to listen.

- Evaluation never ends. You should continue to observe, listen, question and communicate with providers and your child throughout your entire child care experience.

Smart Tips for Parents

- Parents need to periodically evaluate their child care choice.

- Parents should be constantly aware of their children's own impressions and observations about the provider and facility.

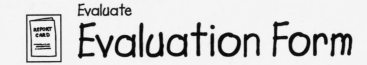

Evaluate
Evaluation Form

American Red Cross

Assign a number from 1 (poor) to 5 (outstanding) for each category, then add your numbers down for a final score.

Category	Evaluation Dates		
	3 Months	6 Months	1 Year
Date			
The Place			
Health and Safety			
Play Area: Inside			
Outside			
Appropriate Toys and Furniture			
Environment: Active Areas			
Quiet Areas			
The Program			
Activities: Fun and Interactive			
Daily Schedule			
Ratios and Group Size			
Art, Music, Sports, Field Trips, etc.			
The Provider			
Experience			
Education			
Relationships: With Adults			
With Children			
Score			

The Quick Search

Under the best of circumstances, you would spend a good deal of time in your search for quality child care. Unfortunately, the real world may not always allow for such detailed, systematic work. You cannot always count on having plenty of time to make your search.

Events can arise that may require that you find child care immediately. What would you do if your center suddenly announced that it is closing in two days? What if your work hours suddenly require a change in providers? What if your long-term provider decides to take an unexpected and extended leave? What do you do then?

Should this happen, be prepared with the following:

Step 1 Research Your Options:
Resource List

Ask friends, family and co-workers for their recommendations. Call your local child care resource and referral agency for a list of child care centers in the area. Make a list of all prospective child care providers and centers. Include each phone number and address. Be willing to add providers and centers to your list as you advance through the search process.

Step 2 Telephone Inquiry:
Telephone Questions

Use the "Telephone Questions" to interview each provider and center. Eliminate the choices that fail the interview or with whom you feel intuitively uncomfortable. A "failed interview" may occur for a number of reasons that range from lack of openings to fees that are too high to concerns about quality.

Step 3 Interview Providers and Centers:
Interview Providers & Centers Outline and Take a Tour
What-to-look-for Guide

After you have narrowed your options using the "Telephone Questions", schedule a time for a meeting with the "finalists." Get a sense for the people and the program. Ask for a daily schedule, written policies and procedures. If it is impossible for you to arrange a visit and you end up enrolling your child via the telephone only, plan to spend some time in the program on your child's first day. *Special note: some programs will not enroll your child without a prior meeting or visit. Skipping the personal meeting or tour is strongly discouraged.*

Step 4 Select the Finalists and Make Your Decision

⟨icon⟩ Put-it-all-together Key

Select a provider or center and make the necessary arrangements to enroll your child. Ask about the center's "probationary period policy". This policy outlines the conditions and time frame within which the parent or program can withdraw the child without a standard advance notice. The policy also addresses the issue of fee refunds.

Step 5 Evaluate

⟨icon⟩ Evaluation Form

After enrolling your child, continue to ask questions, observe and evaluate your decision. If you or your child are not happy or have doubts about your choice, do not hesitate to explore other options.

The search process that we have covered, up to this point, has focused on child care outside of the home. However, some of you might be considering in-home care. The following section will provide you with a step-by-step process in choosing in-home care.

Section V: Finding Quality Child Care: The Search for In-home Care

Section V Goal Statement: When you have completed this section you will identify the steps required in searching for in-home quality child care.

You will be able to:

■ Understand the steps in searching for in-home quality child care

■ Conduct effective interviews of potential in-home child care providers

■ Identify tools to assist you during your search

An Overview of the Search Process

Important steps comprise the search process:

1. Research Your Options:
   ⟨icon⟩ Resource List

2. Interview Providers and Invite Them to Visit Your Home
   ⟨icon⟩ Interview Providers

3. Telephone References:
   ✓ Checking References of In-home Providers

4. Select the Finalists and Make Your Decision
   ⟨icon⟩ Put-it-all-together Key

Smart Tips for Parents

■ Some families may decide at some point during their search for child care to turn to a relative as a provider of child care, or to stay home themselves. These are fine choices that often work well.

5. Evaluate

📄 Evaluation Form

Choosing In-home Child Care

When choosing in-home care, consider the following factors in evaluating a potential in-home child care provider:

- What are the individual's skills?

- What does the individual's mood project to you?

- Is the individual on time?

- Is the individual optimistic?

- Does the individual project a warm feeling toward you?

- How does the individual respond to your child/children?

- Does the individual have a willingness to educate children?

- What is the individual's approach to discipline?

- How does the individual propose to spend his/her time during the day? Will he/she be involved with your child or pursuing his/her own personal agenda?

Your search for in-home child care involves five basic steps, somewhat similar to the steps involved in the other searches for child care. These steps include:

Step 1 Research Your Options:

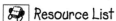 Resource List

Ask friends, family and co-workers for their recommendations. Call your local child care resource and referral agency for a list of in-home care providers in the area. Make a list of all prospective child care providers. Include each phone number and address.

Research Your Options

Resource List
for Choosing Quality Child Care

American Red Cross

Section V
Search Process
Step 1

Date	Name		Phone	Comments
	Address		Contact	

Date	Name		Phone	Comments
	Address		Contact	

Date	Name		Phone	Comments
	Address		Contact	

Date	Name		Phone	Comments
	Address		Contact	

Date	Name		Phone	Comments
	Address		Contact	

Date	Name		Phone	Comments
	Address		Contact	

Date	Name		Phone	Comments
	Address		Contact	

Date	Name		Phone	Comments
	Address		Contact	

Date	Name		Phone	Comments
	Address		Contact	

Step 2 Interview Providers and Invite Them to Visit Your Home

Interview Providers

Use prepared "Interview Providers" questions to help when you speak to potential in-home providers. Eliminate the choices that fail the interview or with whom you feel intuitively uncomfortable. A "failed interview" may occur for a number of reasons.

Before you conduct a telephone interview, have a basic description in hand of the position for which you are seeking help. In addition, build a list of basic information about yourself and your need for in-home child care. The following items may help you build your own list.

- List the days and hours you want in-home care, including vacations and holidays.

- List your expectations including housekeeping, laundry, grocery shopping, errands, and other tasks.

- List any fringe benefits that you may provide such as sick leave, vacation or transportation.

- Mention wages.

- Include the number, names and ages of your children.

- Include the length of time you wish to employ this individual (1 year, 5 years).

After you have narrowed your options using the "Interview Providers" questions, schedule a time for a meeting with the finalists. Invite them one-by-one for an in-home visit. This will allow you to see them in the actual care environment and allows them to obtain a sense of your family, home, yard and neighborhood.

If you determine that you are interested in the individual, you can move forward by asking for references. The points on the worksheet on page 77 will guide you in obtaining detailed information from a reference.

 # Interview Providers

 **American Red Cross**

Name of provider: _____

Below is a list of questions you can refer to when you interview potential candidates.

Questions	Answers
Begin your conversation by supplying the age of your child and the care schedule you are seeking	
1. Why do you want to become a nanny?	
2. What type of parent's helper or nanny position are you seeking, and why do you desire to have this job?	
3. What do you feel is important to the growth and development of a child today?	
4. Please describe any past events which have helped shape your personality in a positive way.	
5. Describe your child care experiences.	
6. What can children within your care hope to learn from you?	
7. What are your future goals and how do you plan to achieve your goals?	
8. What special qualities, skills and training do you have that will make you an outstanding nanny in our home?	
9. What is your philosophy concerning discipline?	
10. What is your approach to discipline? 💡 *Hint: Give an example of a situation in your home with your child to see how the individual responds.*	
11. What sort of relationship do you anticipate between the children and yourself?	
12. How would you characterize yourself to a potential family?	
13. If you were speaking directly to a prospective employer, what comments would you like to make?	

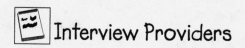
Questions	Answers
14. Do you have CPR and first aid training?	
15. Do you have allergies to animals? (You might consider this if you have pets.)	
16. Are you legally employable?	
17. How would you help a child develop her or his self-esteem?	
18. What would you do if a child comes to you sad? Angry?	
19. How would you respond to a child who challenges you? What would you do?	
20. What would you do if my child were lying to you?	
21. What would you do if there was a fire in the kitchen? In an upstairs bedroom?	
22. What do you feel children need the most from child care providers who work in the family's home.	
23. Why should I hire you over someone else?	
Develop your own questions:	

Step 3 Telephone References

☑ Checking References of In-home Providers

Use prepared "Checking References of In-home Providers" questions on the next page to interview the references provided to you from each potential in-home provider. Eliminate the choices that you feel do not meet your standards.

✓ Checking References of In-home Providers

Name of provider: _____

Use the questions below to check references.

	Yes	No	Explanation
1. Please describe the position and responsibilities this individual had.			
2. Please check "yes" or "no" to each of the following. If any answer is "no", please tell me why.			
easily supervised			
uses own initiative			
any major illness			
good attendance			
team worker			
takes criticism well			
pleasant to be around			
uses good judgment			
prompt			
loyal and honest			
self motivated			
reliable			
active			
works well independently, without supervision			
provides quality care			
3. If you had a position available, would you rehire this individual? Why or why not?			
4. Why did he or she leave your employment?			
5. How long have you known this individual?			
6. What personality traits does this individual have that would make them an exceptional child care provider and role model for children?			
7. Are there any other comments you feel might be helpful?			

Step 4 Select the Finalists and Make Your Decision

Put-it-all-together Key

After checking your references and further narrowing your search refer to the "Put-it-all-together" tool on the next page. This tool will help you to rate your top candidates. After this step you may make your selection and offer the individual the job.

Even if a child care provider receives a high numerical total, that may not be enough to make a decision. Parents must also listen to their "gut feeling" about a provider.

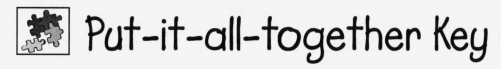 Put-it-all-together Key

Rate your top three candidates in the following categories.
Assign a number from 1 (poor) to 5 (outstanding) to each issue,
then add your numbers down for a final score.

Category	Name of Provider	Name of Provider	Name of Provider
Reference Checks			
Availability			
Past Experience			
Attitude or Approach to Discipline			
Attitude or Approach on Education			
Willingness to Help with Household Tasks			
Interaction with Child			
Has Great Activities for the Child During the Day (daily routine)			
Availability to Take Child to Activities Outside of Home			
Wages			
Has Own Means of Transportation			
Score			

Step 5 Evaluate

 Evaluation Form

After hiring an in-home provider, continue to ask questions, observe and evaluate your decision. If you or your child are not happy or have doubts about your choice, do not hesitate to explore other options.

As you can see from the search for in-home child care, many steps are similar to the procedures for choosing quality child care from a center or family child care provider. The setting you choose for child care is highly individual. What is common to all types of child care is an ongoing need for evaluation and communication with child care providers.

Smart Tip for Parents

You might want to preschedule a three- and six-month face-to-face evaluation with your provider.

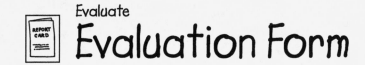 

Evaluate
Evaluation Form

Assign a number from 1 (poor) to 5 (outstanding) for each category,
then add your numbers down for a final score.

Category	Evaluation Dates		
	3 Months	6 Months	1 Year
Date			
Child Appears Happy and Content with Provider			
Provider Appears Happy and Content with Family			
Dependable and On Time			
Handles Feedback			
Attitude or Approach to Discipline			
Attitude or Approach on Education			
Willingness to Help with Household Tasks			
Interaction with Child			
Daily Routine			
Activities for Child Outside of Home			
Keeps Toys Picked Up			
Initiative			
Score			

Section VI: Wrapping It All Up

Section VI Goal Statement: When you have completed this section, you will understand that the quest for quality child care is an ongoing process.

It is a process that includes evaluation and open and regular communications with child care providers.

You will be able to:

- Feel confident in your ability to research and find quality child care

- Understand the need for ongoing evaluation and communication with child care providers

- Realize you are entering into a partnership of trust and commitment with your child care provider or center

Smart Tip for Parents

Start your search by visiting the best child care provider in town. Even if you might not be able to get in, it will give you an idea of good quality child care.

Finding and Selecting Quality Child Care is Just the Beginning

Parents should understand the need for open and regular communications with child care providers. Parents should keep the following points in mind:

- Your job is not to find the "perfect child care provider." Instead, focus on a "good" choice. This approach will reduce your stress and maintain your standards of quality.

- Questions and concerns about child care arrangements should be addressed immediately. Be aware that your child may have an adjustment period when he or she is first enrolled and that separation anxiety can be part of this transition.

- Frequent drop-in visits and observations are a good way to keep informed about the care provided.

- The setting you select for child care has to "feel right." A setting that feels right is the combination of many things: a caring and attentive staff, children who enjoy their child care experiences, and a clean, pleasant environment rich in activities of interest to children.

- If at any time you feel that your needs, as well as those of your child, are not being met, address your concerns right away with your child care provider or teacher.

■ Although searching for quality child care takes time and hard work, the benefits of your efforts are tremendous. In an exciting and interesting learning environment with nurturing, skilled teachers and providers, your child can grow to his or her fullest potential. Your desire to find high quality child care is a gift to your child.

At the beginning of this guide you were introduced to three building blocks, each with the letter "P", which stood for Place, Providers, and Programs .

At the conclusion of this guide, you now know they also stand for something else. By taking a thorough, effective search, you can find quality child care. And through a quality program, your child will have a **pleasant** experience day in and day out. This pleasant experience will be the result of the effective **partnership** in child care that you have formed with your chosen provider. The result? **Peace of mind** that you have made the right choice for your child.

Additional Tools

 # Defining Child Care
From Your Perspective

Child care means different things to different people. Your definition may also change as you work through this guide.

Please take a few minutes to complete the questionnaire below. Once you have defined child care, what you expect to receive from it and fears or reservations you have about it, you can then seek child care providers who meet your needs and expectations.

---

1. To me, the term "Quality Child Care" means:

_____

_____

_____

2. My family will benefit from quality child care in the following ways:

_____

_____

_____

3. My hopes for my child's experience in child care are:

_____

_____

_____

4. My greatest fears about placing my child in child care are:

_____

_____

_____

 # Defining Child Care
From Your Perspective

Child care means different things to different people. Your definition may also change as you work through this guide.

Please take a few minutes to complete the questionnaire below. Once you have defined child care, what you expect to receive from it and fears or reservations you have about it, you can then seek child care providers who meet your needs and expectations.

1. To me, the term "Quality Child Care" means:

_____

_____

_____

2. My family will benefit from quality child care in the following ways:

_____

_____

_____

3. My hopes for my child's experience in child care are:

_____

_____

_____

4. My greatest fears about placing my child in child care are:

_____

_____

_____

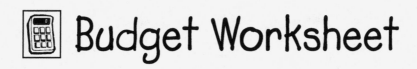 # Budget Worksheet

American Red Cross

Child care costs are calculated, predictable expenses.
Use this worksheet to total your income and expenses.

Income	Current Monthly Income
Net Monthly Income (take home pay)	
Partner's Net Monthly Income	
Other	
Total Monthly Income	A

Expenses	Current Monthly Expense
Mortgage or Rent	
Property Tax	
Transportation: Car payment, gas, tolls, parking, transit	
Utilities: Electric, gas, oil, telephone, water	
Medical Expenses: Doctor, dentist, eye care	
Insurance: Health, car, home/renter's, life	
Credit Card Debt	
Loan Payment(s): Student loan	
Groceries, Dining Out	
Household Items	
Repairs: Home, car	
Cable	
Clothing	
Education	
Entertainment	
Membership Dues: Clubs, unions, civic groups	
Personal: Haircuts, newspapers, magazines, pets, internet service	
Vacations	
Hobbies	
Gifts and Cards	
Charitable Contributions	
Other	
Total Monthly Expenses	B

Additional Expenses Related to Child Care	Expense with Child
Medical: Doctor visits, prescriptions	
Diapering Needs: Diapers (disposable or cloth), wipes, diaper rash cream, diaper service (if needed)	
Nutritional Needs: Formula (if needed), bottles, breast pump, baby food	
Clothing: Clothes, towels, washcloths, bedding, sheets, blankets	
Equipment: Stroller, high chair, crib, changing table, car seat	
Activities: Swim lessons, soccer leagues, etc.	
Activity Supplies: Toys, books, uniforms	
CHILD CARE	
Total Monthly Child Care Expenses	C

Formula

1. Enter Total Monthly Expenses (from **B**)   _____ **(B)**

2. Enter Total Monthly Child Care Expenses (from **C**)   +   _____ **(C)**

3. Add Total Monthly Expenses (**B**) and
   Total Monthly Child Care Expenses (**C**)
   This equals your total monthly expenses with a child (**D**)   =   _____ **(D)**

4. Enter Total Monthly Income (**A**)   _____ **(A)**

5. Subtract Total Monthly Expenses with a Child (**D**)
   from Total Monthly Income (**A**)   -   _____ **(D)**

6. **This total is how much extra money you have available each month.**   =   _____

Helpful Tips

After you have completed your budget, if you find that you have come up short, go back to your Current Monthly Expenses and reconsider some of the following expenses. You may find that you can spend less money on some of these options.

- Dining Out

- Entertainment

- Hobbies

- Cable

- Telephone

- Memberships

- Vacations

- Gifts

- Contributions

- Second Car

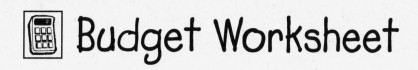 # Budget Worksheet

 **American Red Cross**

Child care costs are calculated, predictable expenses.
Use this worksheet to total your income and expenses.

Income	Current Monthly Income
Net Monthly Income (take home pay)	
Partner's Net Monthly Income	
Other	
Total Monthly Income	A

Expenses	Current Monthly Expense
Mortgage or Rent	
Property Tax	
Transportation: Car payment, gas, tolls, parking, transit	
Utilities: Electric, gas, oil, telephone, water	
Medical Expenses: Doctor, dentist, eye care	
Insurance: Health, car, home/renter's, life	
Credit Card Debt	
Loan Payment(s): Student loan	
Groceries, Dining Out	
Household Items	
Repairs: Home, car	
Cable	
Clothing	
Education	
Entertainment	
Membership Dues: Clubs, unions, civic groups	
Personal: Haircuts, newspapers, magazines, pets, internet service	
Vacations	
Hobbies	
Gifts and Cards	
Charitable Contributions	
Other	
Total Monthly Expenses	B

Additional Expenses Related to Child Care	Expense with Child
Medical: Doctor visits, prescriptions	
Diapering Needs: Diapers (disposable or cloth), wipes, diaper rash cream, diaper service (if needed)	
Nutritional Needs: Formula (if needed), bottles, breast pump, baby food	
Clothing: Clothes, towels, washcloths, bedding, sheets, blankets	
Equipment: Stroller, high chair, crib, changing table, car seat	
Activities: Swim lessons, soccer leagues, etc.	
Activity Supplies: Toys, books, uniforms	
CHILD CARE	
Total Monthly Child Care Expenses	C

Formula

1. Enter Total Monthly Expenses (from **B**) _____**(B)**

2. Enter Total Monthly Child Care Expenses (from **C**) + _____**(C)**

3. Add Total Monthly Expenses (**B**) and
   Total Monthly Child Care Expenses (**C**)
   This equals your total monthly expenses with a child (**D**) = _____**(D)**

4. Enter Total Monthly Income (**A**) _____**(A)**

5. Subtract Total Monthly Expenses with a Child (**D**)
   from Total Monthly Income (**A**) - _____**(D)**

6. **This total is how much extra money you have available each month.** = _____

Helpful Tips

After you have completed your budget, if you find that you have come up short, go back to your Current Monthly Expenses and reconsider some of the following expenses. You may find that you can spend less money on some of these options.

- ■ Dining Out

- ■ Entertainment

- ■ Hobbies

- ■ Cable

- ■ Telephone

- ■ Memberships

- ■ Vacations

- ■ Gifts

- ■ Contributions

- ■ Second Car

Defining Your Preferences

Please circle the letter that best describes your preference.

A. The Basics

1. My child care should be located…
   a) Closer to my house or in my house.
   b) Closer to my workplace.
   c) Closer to my partner's workplace.
   d) Location not critical.
   e) Near public transportation routes.

2. I want to pay for my child care...
   a) As much as my budget will allow.
   b) As little as possible.

3. My schedule is....
   a) Regular. I need child care for my child on the same days for the same hours each week.
   b) Variable. I need flexibility in the days and amount of time my child will be in child care.

B. Your Specific Preferences

4. The Setting:
   a) I like the idea of my child in a home-like setting with just one provider.
   b) I like the idea of my child in a setting designed for children with many providers in the building.
   c) I like the idea of my child being cared for by a provider in my home.
   d) Not sure.

5. Age Considerations:
   a) I want my child to be in a group of children of mixed ages (with a group that could include infants, toddlers, preschool- and school-age children all together with the same provider).
   b) I want my child to be in a group of children of the same age range (all infants in one group, all toddlers in one group, all preschool-age children in another).
   c) I want my child to be cared for alone or just with his or her siblings.
   d) Not sure.

6. Group Size:
   a) I prefer a smaller-sized (less than 8 children) group of children for my child.
   b) I don't mind a slightly larger group (more than 8 children but within the state-regulated group size) of children for my child.
   c) I want one-on-one, individual care for my child.
   d) Not sure.

X+Y=? What Your Choices Mean

A. The Basics:

1. Location: If you answered "A", "B", "C" or "E" you need to consider location seriously when choosing child care. Take a map and mark a radius around your home, workplace or partner's workplace so you know which child care options will fall into your location requirement.

   If you answered "D", location will not be a major factor for you in considering your child care options.

2. Cost: If you answered "A", you probably have already set a budget and determined how much money your budget will allow you to spend on child care.

   If you answered "B", money is an issue in considering child care. You may want to rethink your budget to allow more money for child care. You may also want to check into any benefits your employer may offer for child care. Remember, some child care centers offer scholarships.

3. Schedule: If you answered "A", scheduling will not be much of an issue for you. You will not have much difficulty locating a child care provider who can meet your scheduling needs. Most child care providers prefer you to commit to a regular schedule for your child.

   If you answered "B", scheduling will be an issue as you search for child care. You will need to locate a child care provider who will accommodate your changing schedule.

B. Your Specific Preferences:

If you answered all or mostly "A" to questions 4, 5 and 6, your preferences may lead you to choose family child care as your preferred mode of child care. Family child care offers a home-like setting with usually one provider on-site, a smaller group size and a mixed-age group.

If you answered all or mostly "B", your preferences may lead you to choose center-based child care. Center-based care offers a school-like setting with more providers on site, a slightly larger group size and children are often grouped by age level.

If you answered all or mostly "C", your preferences may lead you to choose a nanny or in-home child care provider. Nannies offer a more individual one-on-one type of care in your home. Nannies often are employed to do light housekeeping duties as well as child care.

If you answered all or mostly "D", you are not sure how to answer these questions. Take time to read through this material when you get home, visit some potential providers and come back to this question again after you have gathered more ideas and information. It is okay to be "not sure" at this time. Some parents may need to look at specific programs before they are ready to make a decision.

Defining Your Preferences

Please circle the letter that best describes your preference.

A. The Basics

1. My child care should be located…
   a) Closer to my house or in my house.

   b) Closer to my workplace.

   c) Closer to my partner's workplace.

   d) Location not critical.

   e) Near public transportation routes.

2. I want to pay for my child care...
   a) As much as my budget will allow.

   b) As little as possible.

3. My schedule is....
   a) Regular. I need child care for my child on the same days for the same hours each week.

   b) Variable. I need flexibility in the days and amount of time my child will be in child care.

B. Your Specific Preferences

4. The Setting:
   a) I like the idea of my child in a home-like setting with just one provider.

   b) I like the idea of my child in a setting designed for children with many providers in the building.

   c) I like the idea of my child being cared for by a provider in my home.

   d) Not sure.

5. Age Considerations:
   a) I want my child to be in a group of children of mixed ages (with a group that could include infants, toddlers, preschool- and school-age children all together with the same provider).

   b) I want my child to be in a group of children of the same age range (all infants in one group, all toddlers in one group, all preschool-age children in another).

   c) I want my child to be cared for alone or just with his or her siblings.

   d) Not sure.

6. Group Size:
   a) I prefer a smaller-sized (less than 8 children) group of children for my child.

   b) I don't mind a slightly larger group (more than 8 children but within the state-regulated group size) of children for my child.

   c) I want one-on-one, individual care for my child.

   d) Not sure.

X+Y=? What Your Choices Mean

A. The Basics:

1. Location: If you answered "A", "B", "C" or "E" you need to consider location seriously when choosing child care. Take a map and mark a radius around your home, workplace or partner's workplace so you know which child care options will fall into your location requirement.

   If you answered "D", location will not be a major factor for you in considering your child care options.

2. Cost: If you answered "A", you probably have already set a budget and determined how much money your budget will allow you to spend on child care.

   If you answered "B", money is an issue in considering child care. You may want to rethink your budget to allow more money for child care. You may also want to check into any benefits your employer may offer for child care. Remember, some child care centers offer scholarships.

3. Schedule: If you answered "A", scheduling will not be much of an issue for you. You will not have much difficulty locating a child care provider who can meet your scheduling needs. Most child care providers prefer you to commit to a regular schedule for your child.

   If you answered "B", scheduling will be an issue as you search for child care. You will need to locate a child care provider who will accommodate your changing schedule.

B. Your Specific Preferences:

If you answered all or mostly "A" to questions 4, 5 and 6, your preferences may lead you to choose family child care as your preferred mode of child care. Family child care offers a home-like setting with usually one provider on-site, a smaller group size and a mixed-age group.

If you answered all or mostly "B", your preferences may lead you to choose center-based child care. Center-based care offers a school-like setting with more providers on site, a slightly larger group size and children are often grouped by age level.

If you answered all or mostly "C", your preferences may lead you to choose a nanny or in-home child care provider. Nannies offer a more individual one-on-one type of care in your home. Nannies often are employed to do light housekeeping duties as well as child care.

If you answered all or mostly "D", you are not sure how to answer these questions. Take time to read through this material when you get home, visit some potential providers and come back to this question again after you have gathered more ideas and information. It is okay to be "not sure" at this time. Some parents may need to look at specific programs before they are ready to make a decision.

Research Your Options

Resource List
for Choosing Quality Child Care

Date	Name	Phone	Comments
	Address	Contact	

Date	Name	Phone	Comments
	Address	Contact	

Date	Name	Phone	Comments
	Address	Contact	

Date	Name	Phone	Comments
	Address	Contact	

Date	Name	Phone	Comments
	Address	Contact	

Date	Name	Phone	Comments
	Address	Contact	

Date	Name	Phone	Comments
	Address	Contact	

Date	Name	Phone	Comments
	Address	Contact	

Date	Name	Phone	Comments
	Address	Contact	

American
Red Cross

Research Your Options

Resource List
for Choosing Quality Child Care

Date	Name	Phone	Comments
	Address	Contact	

Date	Name	Phone	Comments
	Address	Contact	

Date	Name	Phone	Comments
	Address	Contact	

Date	Name	Phone	Comments
	Address	Contact	

Date	Name	Phone	Comments
	Address	Contact	

Date	Name	Phone	Comments
	Address	Contact	

Date	Name	Phone	Comments
	Address	Contact	

Date	Name	Phone	Comments
	Address	Contact	

Date	Name	Phone	Comments
	Address	Contact	

Telephone Questions

Name of provider: _____

Use the questions below to guide your interview with providers or center administrators.
The hints are only to guide you and provide further insight.

Questions	Answers *you receive*
Begin your conversation by supplying the age of your child and the care schedule you are seeking.	
1. Do you have an opening for my child? Do you have any projected openings? 💡 *Hint: If the answer is "no", you do not need to proceed with this center or provider.*	
2. What are the hours and days of operation? 💡 *Hint: Is the program open early and late enough to meet your needs? If not, can you arrange for someone else to drop off or pick up your child? If both answers are "no" you do not need to proceed.*	
3. Where are you located? 💡 *Hint: Determine if the distance from your home or work site is reasonable? Factor in transportation schedules and routes if you take public transportation. If the answer is "no", you do not need to proceed.*	
Note: If the answers for 1-3 are satisfactory and time is limited you may wish to ask if written program information is available. You may review the material at a later time.	
4. What is the daily or weekly rate or cost for my child's schedule? 💡 *Hint: Determine whether you can afford the tuition.*	
5. What additional fees do you charge? 💡 *Hint: Be sure to include in your estimate additional fees charged by the program. Who provides meals or snacks? Who supplies diapers?*	
6. How many days per year is the program closed? 💡 *Hint: It is typical and reasonable for high quality programs to close for major holidays.* Do you charge for closed days? 💡 *Hint: Many family child care (FCC) programs will also close for provider vacations and sick days. Closed days might mean that you pay twice: for child care you do not receive and for alternate care. You must determine what you can afford.*	
7. Is financial assistance available? 💡 *Hint: If tuition costs are too high and no assistance is available, you do not need to proceed.*	
8. Are you licensed, accredited or possess other certifications? 💡 *Hint: This is a an important issue. The center or provider may not be required to be licensed in your state.*	

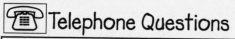

Telephone Questions

Questions	Answers you receive
9. How many children are in your care? *Hint: Large group size or few adults per child translates into less individual attention and supervision per child.* What are the ages of children in your care? *Hint: For center-based providers, ask about adult-to-child ratio and group sizes in your child's age group.*	
10. For family child care: What is your educational background and training? *Hint: Little or no training in child care and development can signal poor quality care.* For centers: How many of your teachers have 2-year or 4-year degrees? *Hint: Programs with staff that exceed minimal licensing requirements for training and education are more likely to provide high quality care.*	
11. For family child care: How long have you been providing care? *Hint: In the child care industry turnover is higher than in many fields.* For centers: How many teachers have been with you more than one year? More than 5, 10? *Hint: Turnover tends to be highest in programs where wages are lowest and working conditions are poorest. High turnover interrupts care and child and staff bonding, and produces stress on staff.*	
12. Do you serve children with special needs? What kinds of specialized training do you (FCC) or staff (center) have to serve the special social, emotional or learning needs children? *Hint: These are important questions if your child has special physical challenges that require special staff training and more individual attention for the child.*	
13. Do you provide transportation? *Hint: This is important if you require help with transportation.*	
14. When can I make an appointment to visit? *Hint: If the provider or administrator is unwilling to allow you to visit and observe it may be a better option to consider other providers or centers.*	
15. Do you have any hand-outs or other written program materials that you would be willing to send me? *Hint: A review of these materials will confirm and validate information from your interview.*	
Write your own individual questions here:	

Telephone Inquiry
Telephone Questions

Name of provider: _____

Use the questions below to guide your interview with providers or center administrators.
The hints are only to guide you and provide further insight.

Questions	Answers you receive
Begin your conversation by supplying the age of your child and the care schedule you are seeking.	
1. Do you have an opening for my child? Do you have any projected openings? *Hint: If the answer is "no", you do not need to proceed with this center or provider.*	
2. What are the hours and days of operation? *Hint: Is the program open early and late enough to meet your needs? If not, can you arrange for someone else to drop off or pick up your child? If both answers are "no" you do not need to proceed.*	
3. Where are you located? *Hint: Determine if the distance from your home or work site is reasonable? Factor in transportation schedules and routes if you take public transportation. If the answer is "no", you do not need to proceed.*	
Note: If the answers for 1-3 are satisfactory and time is limited you may wish to ask if written program information is available. You may review the material at a later time.	
4. What is the daily or weekly rate or cost for my child's schedule? *Hint: Determine whether you can afford the tuition.*	
5. What additional fees do you charge? *Hint: Be sure to include in your estimate additional fees charged by the program. Who provides meals or snacks? Who supplies diapers?*	
6. How many days per year is the program closed? *Hint: It is typical and reasonable for high quality programs to close for major holidays.* Do you charge for closed days? *Hint: Many family child care (FCC) programs will also close for provider vacations and sick days. Closed days might mean that you pay twice: for child care you do not receive and for alternate care. You must determine what you can afford.*	
7. Is financial assistance available? *Hint: If tuition costs are too high and no assistance is available, you do not need to proceed.*	
8. Are you licensed, accredited or possess other certifications? *Hint: This is a an important issue. The center or provider may not be required to be licensed in your state.*	

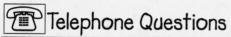 Telephone Questions

Questions	Answers you receive
9. How many children are in your care? 💡 *Hint: Large group size or few adults per child translates into less individual attention and supervision per child.* What are the ages of children in your care? 💡 *Hint: For center-based providers, ask about adult-to-child ratio and group sizes in your child's age group.*	
10. For family child care: What is your educational background and training? 💡 *Hint: Little or no training in child care and development can signal poor quality care.* For centers: How many of your teachers have 2-year or 4-year degrees? 💡 *Hint: Programs with staff that exceed minimal licensing requirements for training and education are more likely to provide high quality care.*	
11. For family child care: How long have you been providing care? 💡 *Hint: In the child care industry turnover is higher than in many fields.* For centers: How many teachers have been with you more than one year? More than 5, 10? 💡 *Hint: Turnover tends to be highest in programs where wages are lowest and working conditions are poorest. High turnover interrupts care and child and staff bonding, and produces stress on staff.*	
12. Do you serve children with special needs? What kinds of specialized training do you (FCC) or staff (center) have to serve the special social, emotional or learning needs children? 💡 *Hint: These are important questions if your child has special physical challenges that require special staff training and more individual attention for the child.*	
13. Do you provide transportation? 💡 *Hint: This is important if you require help with transportation.*	
14. When can I make an appointment to visit? 💡 *Hint: If the provider or administrator is unwilling to allow you to visit and observe it may be a better option to consider other providers or centers.*	
15. Do you have any hand-outs or other written program materials that you would be willing to send me? 💡 *Hint: A review of these materials will confirm and validate information from your interview.*	
Write your own individual questions here:	

 # Interview Providers & Centers Outline

Name of provider: _____

Questions	Answers	Other Information
1. What is your program philosophy? 💡 *Hint: A sound philosophy will help clarify the provider's approach to child care.*		
2. Describe a typical day for a child in your care. (Ask for a copy of the daily schedule.) 💡 *Hint: The program should have a basic daily schedule. Play time should occur in large blocks (at least an hour) during the day.*		
3. What is your policy on discipline? 💡 *Hint: A quality program should not use practices that frighten, humiliate or harm children (examples include spanking, shaming or isolating children or withholding food). Make sure that your child care provider will **never** shake your baby or hit or physically abuse your child. These practices are forbidden by licensing rules in many states.*		
4. How many teachers will each group of children have in a day? Is there a primary lead teacher? Generally, what is the education, training and experience of the care providers? 💡 *Hint: Numbers of teachers or providers per numbers of children is important. Training and experience of care providers is equally important and indicates commitment and professional achievement.*		
5. How many snacks or meals are included? What kinds of foods are provided? Are monthly or weekly menus posted or provided to parents? 💡 *Hint: Meals and nutrition are important for growing children. A good program will have ready answers to these questions.*		
6. What forms need to be filled out and on file? What deposits must be made? Is there a contract to sign? Is there a trial period when starting? How long? 💡 *Hint: Enrollment policies and procedures are important in getting your child into the program.*		

Questions	Answers	Other Information
7. Ask for a set of written policies and a parent handbook. See page 39 for a checklist to review policies at home. Hint: Centers should have written policies. They should be willing to give these documents to you. You should ask about: —withdrawal policies and how much notice needs to be given —late pick-up fees —how the center or provider deals with parent and center/provider vacation days, and —how the center or provider deals with sick children		
8. What are your hours of operation? Hint: Are the hours compatible with your work schedule? How flexible is the provider's schedule? That is, will the provider allow early or late pick-us and drop-offs for special circumstances?		
9. Why should I choose your program?		
10. What distinguishes your program from others?		
11. Additional questions you may have.		

Interview Providers & Centers Outline

Name of provider: _____

Questions	Answers	Other Information
1. What is your program philosophy? 💡 *Hint: A sound philosophy will help clarify the provider's approach to child care.*		
2. Describe a typical day for a child in your care. (Ask for a copy of the daily schedule.) 💡 *Hint: The program should have a basic daily schedule. Play time should occur in large blocks (at least an hour) during the day.*		
3. What is your policy on discipline? 💡 *Hint: A quality program should not use practices that frighten, humiliate or harm children (examples include spanking, shaming or isolating children or withholding food). Make sure that your child care provider will **never** shake your baby or hit or physically abuse your child. These practices are forbidden by licensing rules in many states.*		
4. How many teachers will each group of children have in a day? Is there a primary lead teacher? Generally, what is the education, training and experience of the care providers? 💡 *Hint: Numbers of teachers or providers per numbers of children is important. Training and experience of care providers is equally important and indicates commitment and professional achievement.*		
5. How many snacks or meals are included? What kinds of foods are provided? Are monthly or weekly menus posted or provided to parents? 💡 *Hint: Meals and nutrition are important for growing children. A good program will have ready answers to these questions.*		
6. What forms need to be filled out and on file? What deposits must be made? Is there a contract to sign? Is there a trial period when starting? How long? 💡 *Hint: Enrollment policies and procedures are important in getting your child into the program.*		

Questions	Answers	Other Information
7. Ask for a set of written policies and a parent handbook. See page 39 for a checklist to review policies at home. 💡 *Hint: Centers should have written policies. They should be willing to give these documents to you. You should ask about:* —*withdrawal policies and how much notice needs to be given* —*late pick-up fees* —*how the center or provider deals with parent and center/provider vacation days, and* —*how the center or provider deals with sick children*		
8. What are your hours of operation? 💡 *Hint: Are the hours compatible with your work schedule? How flexible is the provider's schedule? That is, will the provider allow early or late pick-us and drop-offs for special circumstances?*		
9. Why should I choose your program?		
10. What distinguishes your program from others?		
11. Additional questions you may have.		

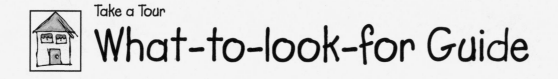

Take a Tour

What-to-look-for Guide

Name of provider: _____

What-to-look-for	Observations
The Place	
■ The environment and materials are clean, safe and in good repair.	
■ The playground is safe and protected from the street. The play area has a thick layer of wood chips or sand underneath. Play structures are not rusted, broken or have exposed areas. Play equipment is secured to the ground and is age-appropriate.	
■ All hazardous materials are stored away from children; poisons, medication, cleaning fluids, matches, sharp tools.	
■ Children are well supervised. They are within the teacher's or provider's sight and sound at all times; ratios and group sizes are at or below state maximums.	
■ Materials are stored where children can reach them: in bins and baskets or on low shelves. Furniture and equipment is child sized.	
The Program	
■ There is a regular daily schedule. Ask for a written copy.	
■ Time is provided every day for outside and inside play; physical activity and quiet play; activities that adults plan; a long period of free play. Meals, snacks and naps (in full day programs can be included). For toddlers and infants, diapering, feeding, and sleeping occur on each child's individual schedule.	
■ Materials are ample and varied. Books; art materials; climbing and riding toys; small and large blocks; dress-up clothes; dolls for pretend play; instruments and music.	
The Provider	
Relationships between adults and children	
■ Adults are warm, friendly and caring with children. Adults regard children as special and provide plenty of smiles and hugs.	
■ Discipline methods are positive and respectful. There is no corporal punishment or any type of frightening or humiliating punishment.	
■ Adults play with children during free play times, sit and talk with them during planned activities and meal times.	

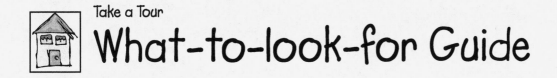

What-to-look-for Guide

Name of provider: _____

What-to-look-for	Observations
The Place	
■ The environment and materials are clean, safe and in good repair.	
■ The playground is safe and protected from the street. The play area has a thick layer of wood chips or sand underneath. Play structures are not rusted, broken or have exposed areas. Play equipment is secured to the ground and is age-appropriate.	
■ All hazardous materials are stored away from children; poisons, medication, cleaning fluids, matches, sharp tools.	
■ Children are well supervised. They are within the teacher's or provider's sight and sound at all times; ratios and group sizes are at or below state maximums.	
■ Materials are stored where children can reach them: in bins and baskets or on low shelves. Furniture and equipment is child sized.	
The Program	
■ There is a regular daily schedule. Ask for a written copy.	
■ Time is provided every day for outside and inside play; physical activity and quiet play; activities that adults plan; a long period of free play. Meals, snacks and naps (in full day programs can be included). For toddlers and infants, diapering, feeding, and sleeping occur on each child's individual schedule.	
■ Materials are ample and varied. Books; art materials; climbing and riding toys; small and large blocks; dress-up clothes; dolls for pretend play; instruments and music.	
The Provider	
Relationships between adults and children	
■ Adults are warm, friendly and caring with children. Adults regard children as special and provide plenty of smiles and hugs.	
■ Discipline methods are positive and respectful. There is no corporal punishment or any type of frightening or humiliating punishment.	
■ Adults play with children during free play times, sit and talk with them during planned activities and meal times.	

👓 Observe the Program
in Action Checklist

✚ **American Red Cross**

Section IV
Search Process
Step 5, Activity #4

Name of provider: _____

What You Want To See	☺	☹	What You Don't Want To See
The Place			
■ If the center or child care home is required to be licensed, the license is posted. There are no licensing violations.			■ The center or home is required to be licensed and the license has lapsed. There are outstanding licensing violations.
■ The environment is clean, safe and in good repair. Outlets are covered; stairways are inaccessible to infants and toddlers; drapery and blind cords are out of children's reach; no chipped or peeling paint; poisonous plants are out of children's reach; and areas have adequate light, heat, and ventilation.			■ Children's areas are dirty, or look unsafe. Some or all of the items listed to the left appear unsafe.
■ Toys and equipment are clean, safe and in good repair. Toys designed for older children (with small pieces) are kept out of reach of infants and toddlers; no toys or equipment have cracked, broken, missing parts, chipped or peeling paint, or sharp edges; toys that have been in children's mouths are set aside and sanitized when children are finished with them.			■ Some or all of the toys and equipment are dirty or in poor condition. Some, or all of the items listed to the left apply to these toys and equipment.
■ In the outside play area, play spaces are separate from walkways; play spaces are separated from bodies of water (preferably by fence, which is required in some states); cushioning is provided under climbing equipment (i.e., pea gravel, wood chips); the sandbox is covered; play spaces are protected from the sun.			■ There is no outside play area, or the area is unsafe. Some or all of the items listed to the left appear unsafe.
■ All hazardous materials are stored away from children; poisons, medication, cleaning fluids, matches, sharp tools.			■ Any hazardous material is found in an area used by children.
■ Age-appropriate safety restraints are used when transporting children (car seats, seat belts).			■ Proper restraints are not used for all children or are not used at all.
■ Sleeping areas are appropriate. Cribs or playpens are provided for infants.			■ Sleeping areas are in adult beds with blankets, quilts and pillows.
■ To reduce the risk of sudden infant death syndrome (SIDS), infants should be put to sleep on their backs.			■ Infants are put to sleep on their stomachs, or care providers are indifferent when it comes to positioning prior to sleep.

What You Want To See	😊	☹	What You Don't Want To See
■ Emergency routes and plans are posted in obvious locations in each room used by children. Fire and tornado drills are practiced regularly.			■ Emergency routes and plans are a mystery; they are not posted in each room used by children. Drills are practiced occasionally or not at all.
■ Emergency numbers for fire, police and poison control are posted next to each phone. Note that not all communities have 911 service.			■ Emergency numbers are not posted, or are not by each phone.
■ Staff and children wash hands before and after eating and before preparing meals, after using the bathroom and after nose blowing. The hand washing area contains plenty of soap and disposable towels or individual cloth towels.			■ Hand washing occurs occasionally or not at all. Hand washing areas run out of supplies. Cloth towels are shared by children and staff.
■ Diaper changing practices. Adults wash hands before and after; soiled diapers are placed in a covered, foot-operated container; diapering surfaces and potty chairs are cleaned and sanitized after each use.			■ Proper diaper changing practices are not followed or are followed inconsistently.
■ Smoking does not occur in areas used by children or in children's presence.			■ Staff are seen smoking in the building, or on-site. Areas used by children smell of cigarette smoke.
■ The classroom or home is clean, attractive and inviting.			■ Classroom or home is dirty or unkempt or may contain unpleasant odors. Note that messes from active play are okay and should not be considered inappropriate.
■ Children have room to play and move around without interfering with each other.			■ The room is crowded. It is either too small or is filled with too much furniture.
■ In centers infant rooms are arranged in areas for eating, sleeping and playing. Toddler, preschool and school-age classrooms also contain areas for art, pretend play, blocks and building, fine motor play and books.			■ No clear areas are visible, or spaces are provided for some, but not all, activities listed to the left.
■ Active and quiet areas are located in different parts of the room or home.			■ Active and quiet play occurs together. The classroom is loud and chaotic with no quiet, protected places for children to be.
■ Children's art work is displayed on the walls. Wall displays are at children's eye levels.			■ Walls are bare or contain only "teacher materials" such as the alphabet, charts, colors. Wall displays are located at adult's eye levels.
■ Materials are stored where children can reach them: in bins and baskets or on low shelves.			■ Materials are stored on closed shelves or on high shelves out of children's reach. Children have to ask for what they want.

What You Want To See	☺	☹	What You Don't Want To See
■ Furniture and equipment is child-sized.			■ Furniture and equipment are too big or too small.
■ Walking children can reach toilets, sinks, changing table and other essential areas on their own (with foot stools when needed).			■ Adults have to place children on toilets. Adults wash children's hands.
The Program			
■ Children are well supervised. They are within the teacher's or provider's sight and sound at all times; ratios and group sizes are at or below state maximums; all people present during the hours of child care have a completed criminal background check; at least one teacher or provider has completed training in handling emergencies (accidents, injuries, fire, tornado); in centers, an adult is available to replace a teacher who is out of the classroom (on break, etc.) Family providers have adults to call on in emergencies.			■ Adults are "clustered" in one area, or are busy with other tasks when children are playing. Any or all of the items listed to the left seem to be apparent.
■ There is a regular daily schedule. Ask for a written copy. Activities happen in the same order each day.			■ There is no regular schedule. Children are not familiar with the schedule and order of activities. The schedule may not be available in written form.
■ Time is provided every day for outside and inside play; physical activity and quiet play; activities that adults plan; a long period of free play when children choose what to do (1 hour or more is good); time for meals, snacks and naps (in full day programs).			■ The activities listed at left do not occur or do not occur every day.
■ For young toddlers and infants, diapering, feeding, and sleeping occur on each child's individual schedule.			■ There is too much adult control, with children in large adult-controlled "lecture groups" for much of the day, or the program looks chaotic: children wander around looking bored with nothing to do, or they run around in groups.
■ Materials and activities are geared to the range of children's skill levels and interests.			■ Materials are for much younger or older children. Children seem bored with the toys.
■ Materials are available during free play times for language (books, story tapes); physical play (riding toys, equipment for climbing); textures (sand, water, modeling clay); fine motor skills (small blocks, puzzles); music (tapes/CDs, instruments). For older children materials are available for art (crayons, markers, scissors, paper); pretend play (dolls, play furniture, dress-up clothes); blocks and building (large wooden blocks, cars and trucks, boards).			■ The classroom or program has few materials or has a lot of one kind of material (blocks) but few or none of another. There may be only one of a very popular toy causing fights or issues with sharing.

What You Want To See	😊	☹	What You Don't Want To See
■ Occasional trips are taken in the neighborhood and community, such as to visit parks, museums, businesses, libraries.			■ The classroom or program does not take field trips. A television is used too frequently as an electronic babysitter.
■ Children have opportunities for learning about differences between people, how to get along together and how to solve problems and conflicts.			■ Differences between people are not discussed. Conflicts and problems are avoided or solved by teachers only.
■ Children with special needs receive the care and attention they require.			■ Children with special needs are segregated from the group, isolated or ignored.
The Provider			
■ Teachers and providers are trained in child development, child care and education.			■ Teachers and providers have little or no formal training.
■ Teachers and providers have experience working with children in an age group for which child care is being sought.			■ Teachers and providers have little or no experience in child care or with the age group for which they provide care.
■ Teachers and providers have good references.			■ Teachers and providers are unwilling to share references or have negative references.
Relationships between adults and children			
■ Adults are warm, friendly and caring with children. Adults regard children as special and provide plenty of smiles and hugs. Staff give children individual attention while aware of needs of the whole group.			■ Adults do not seem to enjoy being with children. Adults ignore or avoid children, or seem generally angry or frustrated with children. Adults are with one child and "forget" the rest of the group.
■ Adults discipline children using words, tone of voice and gestures that are calm, respectful and positive. Note that licensing rules in many states prohibit corporal punishment and any type of frightening or humiliating punishment.			■ Adults yell at, shame or criticize children, use loud voices, use quick or rough gestures such as pulling or pushing. Adults use punishments such as isolating children in a room, threatening or spanking them.
■ Adults speak and listen to children and get down to children's eye levels.			■ Adults do not stop what they are doing to listen to children. Instead, they keep working, walking or talking with others. Adults stand when conversing with children.
■ Adults encourage children to express all feelings. Children are encouraged to express strong feelings safely, without hurting others.			■ Adults do most things for children, or give so much independence that children become frustrated.
■ Adults play with children during free play times. Adults sit and talk with children during planned activities and meal times.			■ Adults play with children only occasionally or not at all, or, supervising play from a distance or completing cleaning or other tasks.

What You Want To See	☺	☹	What You Don't Want To See
■ Children seem to like the teacher or provider and feel comfortable going to them to talk, play or get help.			■ Children appear nervous or uncomfortable. They may avoid contact with the teacher or provider.
Relationships between adults			
■ Teachers and providers are friendly and professional with co-workers and parents. They are sensitive to individual needs and differences.			■ Teachers and providers ignore or avoid parents or co-workers. There is tension or arguing between staff.
■ Teachers and providers share information with parents about their child and his or her activities. They answer parent questions and concerns. Parent conferences occur regularly, once or twice yearly.			■ Parents do not receive regular information about the child or his or her activities. Staff are unavailable or unwilling to answer questions. Conferences are held rarely or not at all.
■ Parents are always welcome to visit. They are encouraged to become involved in the center.			■ Parents are unable or are discouraged from visiting and helping in the class or program.
■ Parents feel comfortable in the center or home. It is the kind of place you would enjoy spending your day.			■ Parents feel uncomfortable, uneasy or unwelcome.

👓 Observe the Program
in Action Checklist

American Red Cross ✚

Section IV
Search Process
Step 5, Activity #4

Name of provider: _____

What You Want To See	☺	☹	What You Don't Want To See
The Place			
■ If the center or child care home is required to be licensed, the license is posted. There are no licensing violations.			■ The center or home is required to be licensed and the license has lapsed. There are outstanding licensing violations.
■ The environment is clean, safe and in good repair. Outlets are covered; stairways are inaccessible to infants and toddlers; drapery and blind cords are out of children's reach; no chipped or peeling paint; poisonous plants are out of children's reach; and areas have adequate light, heat, and ventilation.			■ Children's areas are dirty, or look unsafe. Some or all of the items listed to the left appear unsafe.
■ Toys and equipment are clean, safe and in good repair. Toys designed for older children (with small pieces) are kept out of reach of infants and toddlers; no toys or equipment have cracked, broken, missing parts, chipped or peeling paint, or sharp edges; toys that have been in children's mouths are set aside and sanitized when children are finished with them.			■ Some or all of the toys and equipment are dirty or in poor condition. Some, or all of the items listed to the left apply to these toys and equipment.
■ In the outside play area, play spaces are separate from walkways; play spaces are separated from bodies of water (preferably by fence, which is required in some states); cushioning is provided under climbing equipment (i.e., pea gravel, wood chips); the sandbox is covered; play spaces are protected from the sun.			■ There is no outside play area, or the area is unsafe. Some or all of the items listed to the left appear unsafe.
■ All hazardous materials are stored away from children; poisons, medication, cleaning fluids, matches, sharp tools.			■ Any hazardous material is found in an area used by children.
■ Age-appropriate safety restraints are used when transporting children (car seats, seat belts).			■ Proper restraints are not used for all children or are not used at all.
■ Sleeping areas are appropriate. Cribs or playpens are provided for infants.			■ Sleeping areas are in adult beds with blankets, quilts and pillows.
■ To reduce the risk of sudden infant death syndrome (SIDS), infants should be put to sleep on their backs.			■ Infants are put to sleep on their stomachs, or care providers are indifferent when it comes to positioning prior to sleep.

What You Want To See	☺	☹	What You Don't Want To See
■ Emergency routes and plans are posted in obvious locations in each room used by children. Fire and tornado drills are practiced regularly.			■ Emergency routes and plans are a mystery; they are not posted in each room used by children. Drills are practiced occasionally or not at all.
■ Emergency numbers for fire, police and poison control are posted next to each phone. Note that not all communities have 911 service.			■ Emergency numbers are not posted, or are not by each phone.
■ Staff and children wash hands before and after eating and before preparing meals, after using the bathroom and after nose blowing. The hand washing area contains plenty of soap and disposable towels or individual cloth towels.			■ Hand washing occurs occasionally or not at all. Hand washing areas run out of supplies. Cloth towels are shared by children and staff.
■ Diaper changing practices. Adults wash hands before and after; soiled diapers are placed in a covered, foot-operated container; diapering surfaces and potty chairs are cleaned and sanitized after each use.			■ Proper diaper changing practices are not followed or are followed inconsistently.
■ Smoking does not occur in areas used by children or in children's presence.			■ Staff are seen smoking in the building, or on-site. Areas used by children smell of cigarette smoke.
■ The classroom or home is clean, attractive and inviting.			■ Classroom or home is dirty or unkempt or may contain unpleasant odors. Note that messes from active play are okay and should not be considered inappropriate.
■ Children have room to play and move around without interfering with each other.			■ The room is crowded. It is either too small or is filled with too much furniture.
■ In centers infant rooms are arranged in areas for eating, sleeping and playing. Toddler, preschool and school-age classrooms also contain areas for art, pretend play, blocks and building, fine motor play and books.			■ No clear areas are visible, or spaces are provided for some, but not all, activities listed to the left.
■ Active and quiet areas are located in different parts of the room or home.			■ Active and quiet play occurs together. The classroom is loud and chaotic with no quiet, protected places for children to be.
■ Children's art work is displayed on the walls. Wall displays are at children's eye levels.			■ Walls are bare or contain only "teacher materials" such as the alphabet, charts, colors. Wall displays are located at adult's eye levels.
■ Materials are stored where children can reach them: in bins and baskets or on low shelves.			■ Materials are stored on closed shelves or on high shelves out of children's reach. Children have to ask for what they want.

What You Want To See	☺	☹	What You Don't Want To See
■ Furniture and equipment is child-sized.			■ Furniture and equipment are too big or too small.
■ Walking children can reach toilets, sinks, changing table and other essential areas on their own (with foot stools when needed).			■ Adults have to place children on toilets. Adults wash children's hands.
The Program			
■ Children are well supervised. They are within the teacher's or provider's sight and sound at all times; ratios and group sizes are at or below state maximums; all people present during the hours of child care have a completed criminal background check; at least one teacher or provider has completed training in handling emergencies (accidents, injuries, fire, tornado); in centers, an adult is available to replace a teacher who is out of the classroom (on break, etc.) Family providers have adults to call on in emergencies.			■ Adults are "clustered" in one area, or are busy with other tasks when children are playing. Any or all of the items listed to the left seem to be apparent.
■ There is a regular daily schedule. Ask for a written copy. Activities happen in the same order each day.			■ There is no regular schedule. Children are not familiar with the schedule and order of activities. The schedule may not be available in written form.
■ Time is provided every day for outside and inside play; physical activity and quiet play; activities that adults plan; a long period of free play when children choose what to do (1 hour or more is good); time for meals, snacks and naps (in full day programs).			■ The activities listed at left do not occur or do not occur every day.
■ For young toddlers and infants, diapering, feeding, and sleeping occur on each child's individual schedule.			■ There is too much adult control, with children in large adult-controlled "lecture groups" for much of the day, or the program looks chaotic: children wander around looking bored with nothing to do, or they run around in groups.
■ Materials and activities are geared to the range of children's skill levels and interests.			■ Materials are for much younger or older children. Children seem bored with the toys.
■ Materials are available during free play times for language (books, story tapes); physical play (riding toys, equipment for climbing); textures (sand, water, modeling clay); fine motor skills (small blocks, puzzles); music (tapes/CDs, instruments). For older children materials are available for art (crayons, markers, scissors, paper); pretend play (dolls, play furniture, dress-up clothes); blocks and building (large wooden blocks, cars and trucks, boards).			■ The classroom or program has few materials or has a lot of one kind of material (blocks) but few or none of another. There may be only one of a very popular toy causing fights or issues with sharing.

What You Want To See	☺	☹	What You Don't Want To See
■ Occasional trips are taken in the neighborhood and community, such as to visit parks, museums, businesses, libraries.			■ The classroom or program does not take field trips. A television is used too frequently as an electronic babysitter.
■ Children have opportunities for learning about differences between people, how to get along together and how to solve problems and conflicts.			■ Differences between people are not discussed. Conflicts and problems are avoided or solved by teachers only.
■ Children with special needs receive the care and attention they require.			■ Children with special needs are segregated from the group, isolated or ignored.
The Provider			
■ Teachers and providers are trained in child development, child care and education.			■ Teachers and providers have little or no formal training.
■ Teachers and providers have experience working with children in an age group for which child care is being sought.			■ Teachers and providers have little or no experience in child care or with the age group for which they provide care.
■ Teachers and providers have good references.			■ Teachers and providers are unwilling to share references or have negative references.
Relationships between adults and children			
■ Adults are warm, friendly and caring with children. Adults regard children as special and provide plenty of smiles and hugs. Staff give children individual attention while aware of needs of the whole group.			■ Adults do not seem to enjoy being with children. Adults ignore or avoid children, or seem generally angry or frustrated with children. Adults are with one child and "forget" the rest of the group.
■ Adults discipline children using words, tone of voice and gestures that are calm, respectful and positive. Note that licensing rules in many states prohibit corporal punishment and any type of frightening or humiliating punishment.			■ Adults yell at, shame or criticize children, use loud voices, use quick or rough gestures such as pulling or pushing. Adults use punishments such as isolating children in a room, threatening or spanking them.
■ Adults speak and listen to children and get down to children's eye levels.			■ Adults do not stop what they are doing to listen to children. Instead, they keep working, walking or talking with others. Adults stand when conversing with children.
■ Adults encourage children to express all feelings. Children are encouraged to express strong feelings safely, without hurting others.			■ Adults do most things for children, or give so much independence that children become frustrated.
■ Adults play with children during free play times. Adults sit and talk with children during planned activities and meal times.			■ Adults play with children only occasionally or not at all, or, supervising play from a distance or completing cleaning or other tasks.

What You Want To See	🙂	🙁	What You Don't Want To See
■ Children seem to like the teacher or provider and feel comfortable going to them to talk, play or get help.			■ Children appear nervous or uncomfortable. They may avoid contact with the teacher or provider.
Relationships between adults			
■ Teachers and providers are friendly and professional with co-workers and parents. They are sensitive to individual needs and differences.			■ Teachers and providers ignore or avoid parents or co-workers. There is tension or arguing between staff.
■ Teachers and providers share information with parents about their child and his or her activities. They answer parent questions and concerns. Parent conferences occur regularly, once or twice yearly.			■ Parents do not receive regular information about the child or his or her activities. Staff are unavailable or unwilling to answer questions. Conferences are held rarely or not at all.
■ Parents are always welcome to visit. They are encouraged to become involved in the center.			■ Parents are unable or are discouraged from visiting and helping in the class or program.
■ Parents feel comfortable in the center or home. It is the kind of place you would enjoy spending your day.			■ Parents feel uncomfortable, uneasy or unwelcome.

Put-it-all-together Key

Rate your top three candidates in the following categories.
Assign a number from 1 (poor) to 5 (outstanding) to each issue,
then add your numbers down for a final score.

Category	Name of Center or Provider	Name of Center or Provider	Name of Center or Provider
The Place			
Health and Safety			
Play Area: Inside			
Outside			
Appropriate Toys and Furniture			
Environment: Active Areas			
Quiet Areas			
The Program			
Activities: Fun and Interactive			
Daily Schedule			
Ratios and Group Size			
Art, Music, Sports, Field Trips, etc.			
The Provider			
Experience			
Education			
References			
Relationships: With Adults			
With Children			
Other			
Hours			
Weekly/Monthly Cost*	/	/	/
Meal Plan			
Additional Cost*			
Location			
Score			

*Please refer to back side of sheet

$ Dollars and Sense

Record actual dollar amounts for each option. After you have totaled weekly/monthly cost and additional cost, rate each option. Rate using a number from 1 (poor) to 5 (outstanding).

Factor	Option 1: Hours:		Option 2: Hours:		Option 3: Hours:	
	Weekly	Monthly	Weekly	Monthly	Weekly	Monthly
Regular Tuition						
Extended Care						
Activity Fee						
Meal/Snacks Fee						
Other_____ _____ _____ _____						
Total Weekly/Monthly Cost						
Rate each option on weekly/monthly cost**						
Application Fee:						
Registration Fee:						
Closed Dates: Total number of closed dates that you are charged for, or must pay for: Additional cost to cover alternative child care may need to be considered during these times.						
Total Additional Cost						
Rate each item on additional cost**						

** Copy this rating to front side of sheet.

Put-it-all-together Key

Rate your top three candidates in the following categories.
Assign a number from 1 (poor) to 5 (outstanding) to each issue,
then add your numbers down for a final score.

Category	Name of Center or Provider	Name of Center or Provider	Name of Center or Provider
The Place			
Health and Safety			
Play Area: Inside			
Outside			
Appropriate Toys and Furniture			
Environment: Active Areas			
Quiet Areas			
The Program			
Activities: Fun and Interactive			
Daily Schedule			
Ratios and Group Size			
Art, Music, Sports, Field Trips, etc.			
The Provider			
Experience			
Education			
References			
Relationships: With Adults			
With Children			
Other			
Hours			
Weekly/Monthly Cost*	/	/	/
Meal Plan			
Additional Cost*			
Location			
Score			

*Please refer to back side of sheet

$ Dollars and Sense

Record actual dollar amounts for each option. After you have totaled weekly/monthly cost and additional cost, rate each option. Rate using a number from 1 (poor) to 5 (outstanding).

Factor	Option 1: Hours:		Option 2: Hours:		Option 3: Hours:	
	Weekly	Monthly	Weekly	Monthly	Weekly	Monthly
Regular Tuition						
Extended Care						
Activity Fee						
Meal/Snacks Fee						
Other_____ _____ _____ _____						
Total Weekly/Monthly Cost						
Rate each option on weekly/monthly cost** Application Fee:						
Registration Fee:						
Closed Dates: Total number of closed dates that you are charged for, or must pay for: Additional cost to cover alternative child care may need to be considered during these times.						
Total Additional Cost						
Rate each item on additional cost**						

** Copy this rating to front side of sheet.

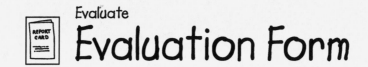 **Evaluation Form**

Evaluate

 **American Red Cross**

Assign a number from 1 (poor) to 5 (outstanding) for each category, then add your numbers down for a final score.

Category	Evaluation Dates		
	3 Months	6 Months	1 Year
Date			
The Place			
Health and Safety			
Play Area: Inside			
Outside			
Appropriate Toys and Furniture			
Environment: Active Areas			
Quiet Areas			
The Program			
Activities: Fun and Interactive			
Daily Schedule			
Ratios and Group Size			
Art, Music, Sports, Field Trips, etc.			
The Provider			
Experience			
Education			
Relationships: With Adults			
With Children			
Score			

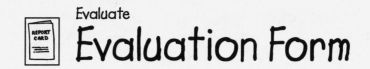

Evaluate

Evaluation Form

American Red Cross

Assign a number from 1 (poor) to 5 (outstanding) for each category, then add your numbers down for a final score.

Category	Evaluation Dates		
	3 Months	6 Months	1 Year
Date			
The Place			
Health and Safety			
Play Area: Inside			
Outside			
Appropriate Toys and Furniture			
Environment: Active Areas			
Quiet Areas			
The Program			
Activities: Fun and Interactive			
Daily Schedule			
Ratios and Group Size			
Art, Music, Sports, Field Trips, etc.			
The Provider			
Experience			
Education			
Relationships: With Adults			
With Children			
Score			

 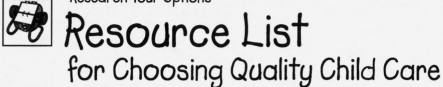

Research Your Options

Resource List
for Choosing Quality Child Care

Section V
Search Process
Step 1

Date	Name	Phone	Comments
	Address	Contact	

Date	Name	Phone	Comments
	Address	Contact	

Date	Name	Phone	Comments
	Address	Contact	

Date	Name	Phone	Comments
	Address	Contact	

Date	Name	Phone	Comments
	Address	Contact	

Date	Name	Phone	Comments
	Address	Contact	

Date	Name	Phone	Comments
	Address	Contact	

Date	Name	Phone	Comments
	Address	Contact	

Date	Name	Phone	Comments
	Address	Contact	

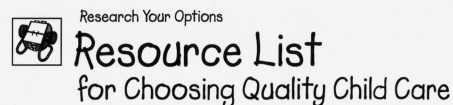

Research Your Options

Resource List
for Choosing Quality Child Care

American Red Cross

Section V
Search Process
Step 1

Date	Name	Phone	Comments
	Address	Contact	

Date	Name	Phone	Comments
	Address	Contact	

Date	Name	Phone	Comments
	Address	Contact	

Date	Name	Phone	Comments
	Address	Contact	

Date	Name	Phone	Comments
	Address	Contact	

Date	Name	Phone	Comments
	Address	Contact	

Date	Name	Phone	Comments
	Address	Contact	

Date	Name	Phone	Comments
	Address	Contact	

Date	Name	Phone	Comments
	Address	Contact	

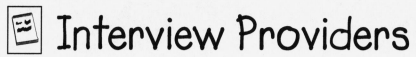 Interview Providers

Name of provider: _____

Below is a list of questions you can refer to when you interview potential candidates.

Questions	Answers
Begin your conversation by supplying the age of your child and the care schedule you are seeking	
1. Why do you want to become a nanny?	
2. What type of parent's helper or nanny position are you seeking, and why do you desire to have this job?	
3. What do you feel is important to the growth and development of a child today?	
4. Please describe any past events which have helped shape your personality in a positive way.	
5. Describe your child care experiences.	
6. What can children within your care hope to learn from you?	
7. What are your future goals and how do you plan to achieve your goals?	
8. What special qualities, skills and training do you have that will make you an outstanding nanny in our home?	
9. What is your philosophy concerning discipline?	
10. What is your approach to discipline? *Hint: Give an example of a situation in your home with your child to see how the individual responds.*	
11. What sort of relationship do you anticipate between the children and yourself?	
12. How would you characterize yourself to a potential family?	
13. If you were speaking directly to a prospective employer, what comments would you like to make?	

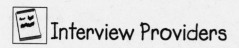 Interview Providers

Questions	Answers
14. Do you have CPR and first aid training?	
15. Do you have allergies to animals? (You might consider this if you have pets.)	
16. Are you legally employable?	
17. How would you help a child develop her or his self-esteem?	
18. What would you do if a child comes to you sad? Angry?	
19. How would you respond to a child who challenges you? What would you do?	
20. What would you do if my child were lying to you?	
21. What would you do if there was a fire in the kitchen? In an upstairs bedroom?	
22. What do you feel children need the most from child care providers who work in the family's home.	
23. Why should I hire you over someone else?	
Develop your own questions:	

 # Interview Providers

 **American Red Cross**

Name of provider: _____

Below is a list of questions you can refer to when you interview potential candidates.

Questions	Answers
Begin your conversation by supplying the age of your child and the care schedule you are seeking	
1. Why do you want to become a nanny?	
2. What type of parent's helper or nanny position are you seeking, and why do you desire to have this job?	
3. What do you feel is important to the growth and development of a child today?	
4. Please describe any past events which have helped shape your personality in a positive way.	
5. Describe your child care experiences.	
6. What can children within your care hope to learn from you?	
7. What are your future goals and how do you plan to achieve your goals?	
8. What special qualities, skills and training do you have that will make you an outstanding nanny in our home?	
9. What is your philosophy concerning discipline?	
10. What is your approach to discipline? *Hint: Give an example of a situation in your home with your child to see how the individual responds.*	
11. What sort of relationship do you anticipate between the children and yourself?	
12. How would you characterize yourself to a potential family?	
13. If you were speaking directly to a prospective employer, what comments would you like to make?	

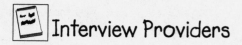 Interview Providers

Questions	Answers
14. Do you have CPR and first aid training?	
15. Do you have allergies to animals? (You might consider this if you have pets.)	
16. Are you legally employable?	
17. How would you help a child develop her or his self-esteem?	
18. What would you do if a child comes to you sad? Angry?	
19. How would you respond to a child who challenges you? What would you do?	
20. What would you do if my child were lying to you?	
21. What would you do if there was a fire in the kitchen? In an upstairs bedroom?	
22. What do you feel children need the most from child care providers who work in the family's home.	
23. Why should I hire you over someone else?	
Develop your own questions:	

☑ Checking References of In-home Providers

Name of provider: _____

Use the questions below to check references.

	Yes	No	Explanation
1. Please describe the position and responsibilities this individual had.			
2. Please check "yes" or "no" to each of the following. If any answer is "no", please tell me why.			
easily supervised			
uses own initiative			
any major illness			
good attendance			
team worker			
takes criticism well			
pleasant to be around			
uses good judgment			
prompt			
loyal and honest			
self motivated			
reliable			
active			
works well independently, without supervision			
provides quality care			
3. If you had a position available, would you rehire this individual? Why or why not?			
4. Why did he or she leave your employment?			
5. How long have you known this individual?			
6. What personality traits does this individual have that would make them an exceptional child care provider and role model for children?			
7. Are there any other comments you feel might be helpful?			

✓ Checking References of In-home Providers

Name of provider: _____

Use the questions below to check references.

	Yes	No	Explanation
1. Please describe the position and responsibilities this individual had.			
2. Please check "yes" or "no" to each of the following. If any answer is "no", please tell me why.			
easily supervised			
uses own initiative			
any major illness			
good attendance			
team worker			
takes criticism well			
pleasant to be around			
uses good judgment			
prompt			
loyal and honest			
self motivated			
reliable			
active			
works well independently, without supervision			
provides quality care			
3. If you had a position available, would you rehire this individual? Why or why not?			
4. Why did he or she leave your employment?			
5. How long have you known this individual?			
6. What personality traits does this individual have that would make them an exceptional child care provider and role model for children?			
7. Are there any other comments you feel might be helpful?			

Put-it-all-together Key

Rate your top three candidates in the following categories.
Assign a number from 1 (poor) to 5 (outstanding) to each issue,
then add your numbers down for a final score.

Category	Name of Provider	Name of Provider	Name of Provider
Reference Checks			
Availability			
Past Experience			
Attitude or Approach to Discipline			
Attitude or Approach on Education			
Willingness to Help with Household Tasks			
Interaction with Child			
Has Great Activities for the Child During the Day (daily routine)			
Availability to Take Child to Activities Outside of Home			
Wages			
Has Own Means of Transportation			
Score			

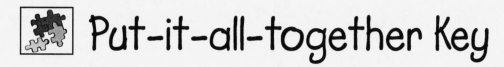 Put-it-all-together Key

Rate your top three candidates in the following categories.
Assign a number from 1 (poor) to 5 (outstanding) to each issue,
then add your numbers down for a final score.

Category	Name of Provider	Name of Provider	Name of Provider
Reference Checks			
Availability			
Past Experience			
Attitude or Approach to Discipline			
Attitude or Approach on Education			
Willingness to Help with Household Tasks			
Interaction with Child			
Has Great Activities for the Child During the Day (daily routine)			
Availability to Take Child to Activities Outside of Home			
Wages			
Has Own Means of Transportation			
Score			

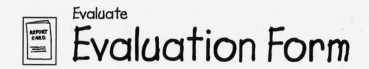Evaluate
Evaluation Form

**American Red Cross**

Assign a number from 1 (poor) to 5 (outstanding) for each category, then add your numbers down for a final score.

Category	Evaluation Dates		
	3 Months	6 Months	1 Year
Date			
Child Appears Happy and Content with Provider			
Provider Appears Happy and Content with Family			
Dependable and On Time			
Handles Feedback			
Attitude or Approach to Discipline			
Attitude or Approach on Education			
Willingness to Help with Household Tasks			
Interaction with Child			
Daily Routine			
Activities for Child Outside of Home			
Keeps Toys Picked Up			
Initiative			
Score			

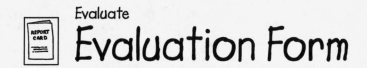

Evaluate

Evaluation Form

American
Red Cross

Section V
Search Process
Step 5

Assign a number from 1 (poor) to 5 (outstanding) for each category, then add your numbers down for a final score.

Category	Evaluation Dates		
	3 Months	6 Months	1 Year
Date			
Child Appears Happy and Content with Provider			
Provider Appears Happy and Content with Family			
Dependable and On Time			
Handles Feedback			
Attitude or Approach to Discipline			
Attitude or Approach on Education			
Willingness to Help with Household Tasks			
Interaction with Child			
Daily Routine			
Activities for Child Outside of Home			
Keeps Toys Picked Up			
Initiative			
Score			